The Long Journey Home

By

Effie Moss

ISBN: 9798633771091 (Paperback)

Front cover image by Artist.
Book design by Designer.

Printed by Amazon - Kindle Direct Publishing in the United Kingdom

First printing edition 2020.

www.effiemoss.com

For Alice

Table of Contents

Prologue:

"If you speak to somebody at the level of the mind, then you speak to the mind.

If you speak from your heart, you will speak to their heart.

But if you speak from experience and life is your story, you will change lives"

Deepak Chopra

August 24th 2014, peering from behind the cushions on my sofa, slightly embarrassed at seeing myself on National TV, I remember my 4 year old little girl, running around, asking why mummy was chatting away on the 32" Plasma screen which filled up our living room.

Alice didn't notice the 5 dragons I was talking to, she didn't spot the 12 minute air time slot, where I answered every possible question that I could about my business. She didn't spot the nerves or the brief moment where I forgot my pitch. To the millions of viewers who watched and supported my episode, it was impossible to see the hoards of people behind the scenes, the camera men, the runners, the crew sitting in the galley just above me. Nobody would have seen the chalked lines I kept stepping over, as I chatted away trying to stop my nerves getting the better of me, or hear the dragons sitting opposite me constantly asking me to step back into my space. After 12 full minutes every viewer saw me secure £50,000 investment for my company. The messages of congratulations flooded in immediately, my platform grew by 80,000 people within 72 hours, my website fell over bringing down 2 million other websites hosted on the same platform, it would have been a dream come true for any start up wanting to leave their mark on the world. But for me, that very moment changed everything.

Dragons Den became the moment which would define the course of events for the next 4 years, events which I found myself completely unprepared for and often trying to understand from a place of total isolation. It would haunt me through my brightest and darkest days. In reality, I made a decision and took action on an idea which changed how I was perceived, the heart of my business and eventually the course of my future. That was the story I told myself.

For 6 years I grew a company founded on a teepee pattern I had created on my living room floor to a global company with a 7 figure revenue stream. Just For Tiny People became the very essence of my existence throughout those 6 years, pulling me into a journey which not only taught me the brilliance and the brutality of start up, it also showed me the value of community and the responsibilities that are intrinsically linked with building an online presence reaching 7 million people a week. Eventually the community I had built came tumbling down around me and with it the company I had put every ounce of my soul into.

Anybody who has built a company and then lost or even sold it may resonate with that period of "quiet" when suddenly the hustle and bustle of start up, just stops. There aren't anymore employees, suppliers or customers to tend to. With a flick of a switch your old world stops and suddenly you are faced with a blank space and the person you have be come looking back at you in the mirror, wondering how you managed to get there and in some cases, like mine, wondering who you are.

As time passed by and I started to reset and heal, reflection became one of my greatest gifts. Looking back, I started to join the dots and began to see that things happened exactly as they were meant to. The people I met, the accomplishments, the learnings, all of it, held a very special gift, one which I could lean into and use to shape my business, my values and the person I wanted to show up In this world as.

Two years ago I stumbled across a video on Gaia called "Finding Joe" I had no idea why I was drawn to it, it simply popped up on my Facebook feed. At the time, I was absorbing so much self development material, trying desperately to understand my purpose, to make sense of all that had happened, I was leaning into the universe, coincidences no longer surprised me, I understood if something crossed my path, I was meant to see it.

Finding Joe became my go to video, whenever I needed to gain momentum. It taught me about the incredible Joseph Campbell and the book he wrote (A hero with a thousand faces) which explains the phases within a heroes journey, a concept which Hollywood story writers still use today and is often seen in the films that grace our screens.

The heroes journey swallowed me up. I became obsessed with the very idea of it. I started to see the many many adventures I had been called to embark upon and when my adventure had finished I always returned back home, a different, more experienced person than the version of myself who had began the journey. I had somehow up levelled to my next level of human.

The call to adventure can arrive in many different ways, occasionally it may be a gentle nudge, a redundancy maybe, a pregnancy, an inspired moment to start a brand new business. No matter how the call arrives, the journey ahead will test the person that you are, it will test your beliefs and the life you have built for yourself. As you move forward, you will strengthen your courage, you will slay your inner dragons and eventually you will complete your adventure and you will return, as a different person, filled with experiences from your journey. It is at this final moment, we generally stop, we move on, the next call to adventure awaits. However Joseph Campbell believed that at the end of every journey we should return back to our community to share our story.

It is only at the point when we release the knowledge that we have gained and we share our story with others, that our experiences can truly matter. Inspiring and enabling others to take a deep breath and put their best foot forward. I fundamentally believe that there is a reason why we have the platforms available to us to share stories and encourage phenomenal conversations. Podcasts, Blogs, Online Communities, filled with stories from ordinary people who have embarked on an incredible adventure and returned back to their community to share their story.

When we take the time to listen to another's story, we hear their truth, a truth, which has the power to change lives. Listening helps us to become more empathetic, it fills us up with with appreciation, helping us to understand the essence of courage and often we are inspired to do more. The story becomes the call to every human being who has been given the privilege to show up in this world, to take action within their lives. It is also a reminder, to fall over, but to never ever deny yourself the ability to bounce back. Your story will be your greatest gift to the world, it is YOUR story, filled with every single part of your souls journey as a human being.

If I think back to all of the adventures I have had during the past 42 years, I think of the random people I have met, those who I am so lucky to call my friends, people I have loved and still very much love. I think of the brilliant conversations I have had, the IVF journey I embarked on which gave me my very best gift, my incredibly smart, beautiful Alice.

I think of my strict Greek childhood filled with domestic violence which taught me an inner strength I have continued to call upon throughout my life. I think of the men and women in my life who have tried to keep me small and in the same breath I think of the many men and women in my life who have lifted me up.

Amongst my adventures some of my greatest lessons came from the ups and downs of the business I loved and had the absolute privilege of creating an enormous impact with. The journey that followed took me on a path of self discovery and helped me to find a deeper connection with myself. I relearnt how to belly laugh again and find genuine joy in the world around me. I was reminded of my love for community and story and how to make lemonade with the lemons I was dealt with. I have shown up in this world, not always at my best, but as a human being always willing to learn and grow.

This book is my story. It has been hiding inside of me for many years and finally the tight feeling in my throat I get every time I think of writing it, reminds me that it is time to release my fear and respond to my next adventure. I wrote it initially to share with my Alice, to help her understand that when Life hands you juicy lemons, the ability to bounce back lies within you and only you.

I want Alice to know, that nobody has the right to keep you small or to affect the way you live your life. I want her to stand in front of the mirror and know with absolute certainty who is looking back at her. I want her to see strength in her body and in her mind, I want her to trust her voice and use it with confidence and conviction. I want her to know that when she is knocked down, she has everything inside of her to lift herself back up. But ultimately I want her to understand that kindness matters above anything else. A kind word, a genuine smile, a gesture from the heart, they all have the ability to make this world a better place.

As I have written this book, it has become apparent to me that the very same words I want to share with my daughter, may resonate with you. I hope amongst the following chapters you will find your own joy and the courage to follow the path that is destined to be yours and when you need to find the strength to bounce back, you only need look inside of yourself.

There is no shame in my story or in any part of yours. It may feel like there is at times, we all fear judgement, that is part of being human, however the moment you let your story control you, you lose the ability to see the lessons you were gifted in this lifetime.

Lead the life you so very much deserve. Own your story and use your incredible voice to share your experiences. Somewhere, out there, there is somebody who needs to hear the very words you have to share and I promise you, when they do, it will change their lives forever.

Much Love

Chapter 1: Growing up

"I am not what happened to me, I am what I choose to become"

Joseph Campbell

When I was 11 years old, I found myself running through a very quiet street with a silver Mercedes chasing me. It was late at night and most of the houses that layered the street had their curtains drawn. It was the era of the net curtains with the heavy pelmet curtain overlay. The thickness of the fabric would mute any sound and as we lived at the end of a quiet road, drama was very rarely found late at night.

I remember the fear that coursed through my veins, as I pushed myself to run faster and faster, I remember focussing ahead until I eventually jumped a garden wall and found my-self hiding amongst a neighbours bushes. I was 11 years old, I should have been asleep in my bed, I shouldn't have been running for my life being chased in a car by a man, who was meant to love me, simply because I had stepped between his fist and my beautiful mum. My childhood was filled with so many dramatic memories, some I can recall and some I cant. Over the years I have suppressed so many memories I have no idea if this was the worst incident or how many similar events there were.

My dad bought our house when I was 6 years old. I have little memory of my life before our move to Camborne Road, I remember being told that my dad had bought the 3 bedroom semi detached house in Raynes Park, he came home one day and told my mum we were moving. There may have been a number of viewings, there may have been mortgage conversations or even school conversations, however those were only for the eyes and ears of the 'man of the house'.

My mum married my dad when she was 17 years old, he was 11 years her senior, it was a typical greek match, she was running way from a strict greek upbringing and ran straight into the arms of a man who only knew how to show his love through his fists. Within a few weeks of marital bliss she was blessed with the news that she was expecting a baby. I was born 5 days after her 18th birthday, a little yellow and very small at 5lbs 11oz, my sister followed by her 19th birthday and by her 21st she had 3 children under 4. By her 26th birthday my brother arrived, producing the heir my dad had craved for.

Christmas's in A&E, Police Sirens, jumping out of the ground floor bay windows in our house, running to neighbours to find safety, the screaming and the banging of doors, the arrests and over night stays in the police to separate him from my mum, the nights we spent sleeping in a car in a Macdonalds' car park or next to Motspur Park train station dogged my childhood. For some reason these are the memories I remember, they are the ones which have stayed with me as I met my husband and brought my little girl into the world. When I look back it has become clear to me that the street lamps taught me to feel safety when light shines over darkness. Inner strength, strengthened from the worst possible moments enabled me to push forward and pursue my dreams. It formed a hunger inside of me to do better, to be independent and never ever believe the word no.

When I was 8 years old, I had an idea to make friendship bracelets out of yarn. I remember plaiting the bracelets at night before I went to bed, the next day I would hide them in my desk at school. I feel so incredibly old as I remember back to those wooden square desks with lids, which opened up, hiding the compartment where you stored your books and pencils, often scratched with the names of those who had been before us. Thankfully as I got older those desks were replaced with tables, similar to those that Alice sits at now at school. Amongst the pencils hid my first ever product, my friendship bracelets. Every lunchtime I would bring them out and sell them for pennies. This was my first business venture and possibly where my love for product came from, the idea of creating something from nothing and using it to make people happy, filled me up, it still does.

I vaguely recall a teacher finding out about my underground venture and telling my mum. Entrepreneurship wasn't a "thing" when I was younger, it wasn't widely understood. Bill Gates hadn't launched Microsoft, the Apple Computer was unheard of and the idea that you could run your own business and earn a living was unfathomable. People found safety in their jobs, most thought they were set for life, business was meant for the generations who had them deep rooted in their history.

Except it seems for my family. My dad ran his own business he was a mechanic and ran several successful garages, even at a young age I could see the toll it took on him. I watched the late nights and the hard work he put in to create a business which fed and clothed us, entrepreneurship ran in my blood and as I look at my siblings now, who all own their own successful businesses, I guess the apple, in this case didn't fall too far from the tree. When the teacher told my mum about my new venture, that was the end of my first ever small business.

I remember this story, simply because of the way it had made me feel. I have so much pride knowing that even at 8 years old the sparks of what would become my entrepreneurial journey had started to show themselves. It makes me smile even now, 34 years later. I often wonder if I had been allowed to keep my business, would it have stopped my incessant obsession with approval. I have a feeling I remember this point of my childhood because it was likely the very moment that two seeds were planted.

The first was my love for business, to build something of my own and to know that I could.

The second however is a little more complicated and is related to childhood trauma and valuing my own self-worth, that good old chestnut. I sought safety in my achievements, I had full control over how I showed up and performed, but as with all achievements there is a thin grey thread which attaches itself to you self worth. Low self esteem pushes you to constantly seek approval from those closest to you. No matter how long your list of accomplishments you never fully feel whole until you receive that well done from the one person you have tried to show up for over and over again, in my case it was my dad.

This stayed with me until for almost 40 years, when I finally faced the trauma hidden inside of me, I found the courage to look my self worth straight in the eye and know that I was enough just as I was. Everything I knew and had journeyed through had made me the person I am today. I no longer needed to relive my childhood over and over again, subconsciously or consciously. It was safe and perfectly ok to leave the events of my childhood behind me.

For now I had still so much to learn and somehow this early memory made me feel unworthy, thinking it was the right thing to do, my teacher and my mum ended my first ever business, little did I know that very decision, lay deep rooted until 2017 when my greatest fear came into fruition and played out almost perfectly in my reality.

I would also like to take a moment to mention that, as an adult, often embarking into unknown territory, I completely understand the decision that was made. We make decisions based on the knowledge and experiences we have at that time. What may have seemed right in that moment is very rarely driven by somebody's need to cause harm. My mum did what she thought was best, she wanted me to abide by the rules and my teacher wasn't familiar with a child entrepreneur or how to recognise the signs. They both did what they thought was best. I am sure I make decisions now regarding Alice which I will very likely question as she grows into an adult. Hindsight is a wonderful thing, the good news is that we have a choice at any moment in our lives to continue to feed an old story or create a new one.

My childhood years were the years I had no control over, I recognise that my will to live a better life than the one I was born into, deep rooted itself inside of me from very early on. The domestic violence incidents happened much more regularly as we grew up, eventually they turned to me too. I was so angry, especially during my teen years, I had a voice, which was often wrought with emotion, unfortunately when you throw emotion into the mix, very rarely is the core message heard. In my case it was 'help.' A policewomen once warned me that if I didn't stop screaming at my dad, she would arrest me too. I was 14 years old and had just watched him use my mum as a punching bag, dragging her by her hair down a flight of stairs and here I was being reprimanded for acting out through the trauma I had not long before, witnessed.

Even after the nights we had slept in the car, we still got up everyday and made our way to school. We showed up, we attended all of our classes and we swallowed up as much knowledge as we could. We learnt and studied and even though the A's were never good enough, I knew inside of me that I was building a foundation I could build the rest of my life upon. Funnily enough it would be my education I would call upon several times in my adulthood to pick me back up and enable me to reset.

The night before my english G.C.S.E exam a huge fight exploded between my mum and dad, I can't recall what it was over, very likely money, it normally was, mainly because he was also a gambler. I remember jumping in the centre of the fight and the next thing I knew I was being told to leave and to pack up my bedroom. My mum drove me to my grandparents house to stay that night and the next day I sat my G.C.S.E english exam. Thankfully I passed all of my G.C.S.E's, yet to this day I have no idea how I did it. I learnt how to compartmentalise my feelings to ensure I remained focussed. These were the years that I dreamt of a peaceful life, full of choices and a business I could call my own. It was also during these early years, that I learnt the value of routine.

Routine, became the reason to get out of bed, school kept me moving. Even on the days when my feet felt heavy underneath me, when I would cry my heart out, wishing and hoping for a different life, I learnt that the only person who could change my situation, was me. At every point of my life when I have faced adversity, the ability to flick the switch and turn it around, always lay with me. It was a lesson I learnt from a very very young age and one I would call upon more times than I can count, during the course of the years ahead.

When my wonderful business closed its doors many many years later, it would be the simple routine of getting up out of bed and taking Alice to school, waiting until 4pm to collect her, bring her home, cook dinner, read a story and pop her to bed, which would again help to build the foundation in myself where I could begin to reset and start the journey ahead of bouncing back. If you were to ask Alice now, how I spent those two years following the closure of JFTP, she will tell you I was busy being a mummy. For the first time since she had been born I had stopped, I was present and whilst I was trying desperately to heal the many many cracks which had formed, I clung onto our routine to ensure I kept moving forward.

The days weren't easy, some were very hard, I carried an awful lot of guilt and at the time, shame. I was confused and lost and I didn't recognise the person staring back at me in the mirror. I was grieving for a world I had built and a business which had encapsulated my heart from the very moment I had conceived it. I grieved for the loss of our beautiful home, our financial stability and the fact that I had let so many people down, including those I loved deeply. I hated myself more than the abuse I was receiving online or the hate mail I would find in my inbox on a day to day basis. I didn't quite know how to make peace with myself.

Those first few months, where I simply existed, it was my Alice and our daily routine which kept me moving. I had a reason to get up every single day and take the small steps needed to stop the darkness from swallowing me up and believe me when I say, the nights were the worst, the conversations you can have with yourself when you are deep in depression and the night sky is black and you have stopped searching for the stars, can be pretty scary.

If you are reading this and life has given you a knock, firstly I am so sorry that you are in a place where you are feeling anything but joy. I promise that as the old saying goes "time heals old wounds" however if you are anything like me, you just want to figure it out right now, contemplating the idea that you will have to feel the feelings that you currently feel for any longer than you have to, doesn't bare thinking about.

Please know that you have permission to feel every feeling that you have. You have permission to cry and scream and yell at the world. Pour your thoughts into a journal, share with a friend or a loved one, jump onto a helpline and speak to a kind stranger, please do not bottle anything up, do not lock it away and pretend it doesn't exist. Your mental health deserves better and so do you.

Your call to adventure will challenge you beyond what you think you are capable of, but know that the universe will never give you more than you can deal with. You are growing and as painful as it may feel you are levelling up to your next level of human, you are evolving and becoming an even better version of you. You have to be, you know more than you did yesterday and less than tomorrow, you are evolving.

However in doing so, you must also move. You must get out of bed and find a reason to walk outside, walk to a coffee shop, meet a friend, walk a friends dog, it doesn't matter. Please keep moving every single day, no matter how hard it can feel at times. Show up in the world as your beautiful self and know that you have everything inside of you to enable you to heal and bounce back. As the wonderful Mel Robbins says, count 5-4-3-2-1 and move!

Eventually you will find the strength to look up and as each day passes you will find that you have taken a step further, it may have been a teeny tiny step, but you will find that your routine has helped you to rebuild a foundation you can build your life upon.

It took me many years to even attempt to understand the abuse my beautiful mum suffered at the hands of a man who was convinced that he loved her so much that he needed to control her and in doing so the only way he knew how was through the use of his fists.

I have watched her rebuild her life in a completely different country and whilst she has faced challenges, she has grown as a person and through it all has become incredibly funny and kind. There is a peace to her past which I admire. The years which were haunted with depression are far and few between now. She was married to my dad since she was 17 years old for 25 years, she had to relearn how to look after herself, earn her own money and learn who she was outside of her role as a wife and a mum to the 4 of us.

You could argue that she should have left him earlier and maybe yes she should have. I have thought about it a great deal over the years and every time I arrive at the same conclusion, it wasn't the right time for her. The time did come and at a point when we were older and we could help. Never have I regretted anything as much or felt more empowered than the day he came to me asking me to convince her to come home. The words that fell out of my mouth were hurtful and hateful, I was 22 years old and it hadn't dawned on me that treading a path of forgiveness lightens your heart and helps you to move forward with the lessons you have learnt. To this day I am still not sure if I was standing up for my beautiful mum or the very scared child he had taken her childhood from.

I am now 42 years old and 20 years have passed, the years have not shown my dad kindness, he suffers from a heart condition and refuses to have a heart surgery. He chooses fear above life and in doing so tells me so much about the man he continues to be. I can think of my childhood now without the pain I once knew, I have come to accept that he was a product of his own environment and upbringing and the choices he made were based on the experiences that he had endured in his life. His passionate need to love drove his need to control. I am not condoning his behaviour in anyway or justifying the hurt that he caused, I am choosing to recognise it for what it was and allowing forgiveness into my heart. In doing so, I have also recognised that a generational cycle has been broken.

The history that dogged my family will no longer exist in our future, our children are now free of the childhood we had. They know only love and stability and a fierce resolve to do the very best by them. I also accept that from a very young age I had to learn how to show up in this world and how to use my voice to be heard. My determination to be an independent women was born from my fear of living the life my mum had. My relationship with my husband was formed from the very same foundation and I can honestly say that despite everything, I have the capacity to find peace in what has been and to also forgive and to love.

Forgiveness comes from doing your inner work and exploring trauma within your life. Work you have to do to accept past events and learn how to make peace with the events that haunt you. In order to do that though, you have to meet yourself exactly where you are. That is the only starting point that you have. Your will to change, to release the past will empower you beyond measure but first you must stand in front of the mirror and peer into your soul and accept all that you are. When you are able to do that, the people who have tried to hurt you will lose their control over you. Simply because you have started to get to know you. You have given yourself a gentle nod and quietly acknowledged "I see you" and that my friend, is so incredibly powerful.

You have the absolute right to show up in this world as your wonderful authentic self. Smell the gorgeous pink roses, dance in the rain, call a friend you haven't spoken to in a while. Chat to the person standing next to you on the train, love freely and take a step forward, be brave and start that business you have been dreaming of. The stars were aligned when you entered this world, they shine upon you every single day because they believe in you, please don't waste another moment thinking you are any less than you absolutely deserve to be.

The trauma I experienced during those early years of my life, shaped the adult I grew into, which includes my ability to feel very deep emotion. I cry easily, not because I am weak, but because my ability to feel and be empathetic has been heightened due to the experiences which crossed my path as a child. I hate saying goodbye, I will cry a river of tears when I have to say goodbye to somebody I have felt a deep connection with.

When the tears have dried and I have taken a step back, I realise that I am saying good-bye to a part of my adventure and I acknowledge that I am so much better for having known the incredible people who have been part of my journey.

Joseph Campbell mentioned that throughout the heroes journey you will meet many people who will help you on your journey. I believe that every person we have the privilege to meet helps us to reach our next level of human. Be kind, have patience and in this world where we can type hurtful things faster than our ability to calm down, take a moment and breathe. The way you make somebody feel has a far bigger impact than the words you think you want to share.

It could be a stranger from the train, who you chat about the weekend with, or a friend from work who you have gotten to know so well that in many ways they have helped you to heal just by being themselves. It's the smashed avocado and scrambled egg breakfast you fell in love with during the days you had to travel away from home. It could be the belly laughs you have when you watch something from afar or the simple thank you, you receive just by showing up and extending kindness to somebody who simply needed a hug. Every person, every conversation and story has a place in your adventure and will propel you forward to your next chapter. As you fly forward do so with open arms and a grateful heart and feel excited about the life you have ahead.

At the end of last year I was sitting on a Virgin Atlantic flight on my way to Boston for a week long training session for the company who had just hired me. I was feeling a little confused as I had stepped off my entrepreneurial path and whilst the thought of working was exciting, it had given me a new lease of life and a purpose, I was questioning if I would ever go back into my old world. It didn't make sense to me that through everything I had learnt and experienced I wouldn't return back to the entrepreneurial world. A mentor advised me to take the time and reset and so I jumped onto the flight eager to please the new company who had hired me.

As fate would have it, sitting next to me was a young man called Joe. Joe was from Boston, living in the UK, he was travelling home for Christmas. As we started to chat, I learnt about Joe's career and the amazing adventure he had been on during the past few years. I also learnt about his growing need for change.

There was nobody more perfect to sit next to for a 7 hour flight. After 4 1/2 hours of constant chatter and laughter we decided to stop talking, rest, watch a film and pick up in a short while. I felt a deep connection with Joe and whilst we chatted, I shared my business story, every part of it, even the hairy parts. For the first time in 18 months, I stood by my story and owned it, rather than let it own me. It was in that moment that I realised that I was on my way to making peace with the previous 18 months and the reason I was sitting on the plane, on my way to Boston was simply because that was exactly where I was meant to be.

My daily routine, accepting where I was and moving from that point, staring into my soul and working out who I was, somehow it had all come together and in that very moment I realised that I was bouncing back. Whilst my path looked different to the one I had hoped or envisaged for myself, for whatever reason, this was the path I was on. I could either accept the opportunity in front of me or resist it. I knew better than to resist something the Universe had perfectly aligned.

Joe and I stayed in touch following our time on the flight, I couldn't be more proud of the courage he showed during the course of the following months. He resigned from his job, moved from the UK to Berlin, found a friend to stay with and embarked on a new adventure. He has shown so much courage and ambition to go after his dreams. On that very cold December day on our way to beautiful Boston, he reminded me to show up for mine.

And so what does all of this have to do with the business I went on to build?
In all honesty, everything.

The foundations of my childhood, fed the mindset I led with in my business. The passion that grew in my heart to build my own company from those very early days when I first made a friendship bracelet, fuelled the product based company that I eventually grew. Routine enabled me to push through the harder days and trauma shaped how I chose to use my voice.

And Joe?

Well Joe was one of the very first people who took my story at face value, without any judgement and in a very quiet, subtle way helped me to embrace every part of my story and move forward.

Chapter 2: Creating JFTP:

"If the path before you is clear, you are probably on someone else's"

Joseph Campbell

Often when I sit and reflect on my JFTP journey, I am reminded how far an adventure can take you, in such a short space of time. Starting a business is such a significant step, it not only impacts you directly, but those around you too. It's safe to assume that during JFTP's tenure I was very rarely present and didn't spend a great deal of time with my family. My body was present, my mind on the other hand was always pre-occupied with a million things I needed to do.

It is very true what they say "being an entrepreneur is hard, if it were easy, everybody would do it" I still hold onto the ideal that a business can impact the world in ways that employment may not be able to. A brash statement I know, but one I believe in simply because I have held careers in both worlds. The only difference between a 9-5 corporate job and the job that you create for yourself, is the limitless ceiling. Both roles have the ability to keep you small, to feed those self doubt niggles, to drain away your joy, but they can also lift you up, inspire you and place you in the company of like-minded people.

A limitless ceiling is created the very moment you decide to create a business, there isn't a glass ceiling to smash through, it just doesn't exist. Which essentially means that you can change the course of your journey at any one point. You can create a new product or service because you want to, you can rebrand and refine your message, you can choose the path to acquire funding, simply because you can. And there lies the freedom that many entrepreneurs often look for when creating a business they can call their own.

Just For Tiny People began it's life as Just For Alice, it was an idea I had formulated in my head whilst working full time at Marks & Spencers, launching the first release of their £300 million multi channel program. The two worlds couldn't have been more different or even less inspired. My 9am - 5pm was a 7am - 9pm job, 5 days a week. I was a new mummy, leaving my 1 year old Alice at home with daddy and grandma to be looked after. Like so many people, this wasn't the life I had envisaged for myself, as a women or as a mother. I wanted something different and this time I knew that I needed to set a different example.

How could I tell Alice to go after her dreams, if I didn't go after mine?

I sometimes feel when reflecting back on the early days this story there may have been an explosive start, a grand gesture in starting a company which would eventually take me on such a significant journey, but JFTP was actually created on my living room floor - literally! JFTP's story was that of very very humble beginnings amongst a reality, that many people, I am sure, can identify with.

I had seen an adult wigwam in a textile book on a family weekend trip to Seaview on the Isle of Wight. My head was full of business ideas and I had given myself such a headache trying to force the next big idea. When I relaxed and leaned into my thoughts, allowing them to guide me, I found myself in a gift shop, with a big white hardback textile book in my hand. As I flicked through pictures of cushions and stuffed toys, a colourful adult wigwam jumped out at me. I could instantly see Alice sitting inside this huge Teepee like tent, playing with her toys, I could see us both sitting inside reading and playing. In that very moment I closed my eyes and took a step forward on a path that I had absolutely no idea what to do with. That very excitable moment literally changed the course of my life. On that sunny Saturday in Seaview, I committed to making Alice a teepee, but more than anything it felt like fun, even though I hadn't sewn in 20 years and so I decided to follow joy.

I should mention at this point that at 33, I hadn't sewn since I had left school. I hadn't touched or threaded a sewing machine for almost 20 years, not to mention sew a straight seam. I didn't know anything about fabric types, patterns or seam allowances. But how hard could it be? So I ordered my very first Janome sewing machine from amazon and with a picture in hand of the wigwam which had inspired me, I started a 12 week journey, sewing every night after work to create my first ever Teepee for Alice.

After 20 metres of plain calico and 5 metres of dotty cotton fabric, my teepee stood tall on 4 oddly shaped bamboo poles I had bought from B&Q. Reflecting back it was amazing how imperfect everything was. The teepee pattern I had used to cut the fabric with, was made from 20 pieces of A4 plain paper cello taped together on my living room floor.

The wonky stitching on the teepee was part hand stitched and part machine stitched. I had taught myself how to thread the sewing machine using a youtube video online. There was nothing about this that screamed a million pound business or that I even had an idea how to create a handmade product business. It didn't feel like a Dragons Den investment worthy business or provide the slightest inkling that this one teepee would go on to help build a community reaching 7 million people a week. For 4 months, my wonky teepee sat in my living room, home to Alice and her teddy bears, we played, we read, we imagined and for those wonderful 4 months I saw the world through the eyes of my little girl.

JFTP was born out of an aspiration to create as many magical memories as I possibly could, through a product I wholeheartedly believed in. Over the years I had the privilege to create tens of thousands of Teepees shipped around the world. At no point were my Teepees tents, fabric on sticks or wigwams. I always believed and still do, that every teepee created a magical space for children to imagine their world, to play and explore, a space where a child could just be a child. There was something pure and fun in the simplicity of the whole idea, it fills my heart up knowing that even today, there are still JFTP teepees creating magical memories out there in the world.

JFTP's explosive growth was as a result of two very clear things. The first was timing, we entered the market at a time when the product was in its infancy and we had the opportunity to lead the market and shape the product. The second was purpose. Every teepee was made to create the memories we would all want for our children and in some ways for ourselves.

I lost count of the amount of times over the years somebody would ask me if an adult could fit inside our teepees too. We all want to feel like a child again, how amazing would it be to lie on our backs in the grass and cloud watch, build dens out of clothes airers and truly believe that we could travel back in time with Marty McFly. JFTP provided a sense of belonging to something idealistic which was greater than ourselves. Given my childhood, it is no surprise that I had concentrated on the magic missing from my own world growing up and so instead I invented a world which would have existed exactly as I would have hoped it could - and for almost 6 amazing years, it did.

At the peak of my lovely business, my online community reached 7 million people a week. 7 million incredible people would see my company pop up in their feed on a daily basis. My wonderful company was creating a worldwide impact. Despite popular belief my interest wasn't financial, I don't think I ever talked about wanting to make lots of money, I was very clear on the mission for my company. I wanted to impact the lives of tiny people and help families create memories which would help shape their childhood, memories I knew, would provide a solid emotional foundation for the adulthood that was to come.

Growing and giving birth to my little girl shaped a very clear idea in my head as to how I wanted her childhood to develop. I wanted Alice to know that more than anything that she is incredibly loved and I wanted to make sure that she would always feel safe and secure. I knew that the childhood memories we created with Alice would provide her with the basis to build her adulthood on.

The idea of a teepee as a fully fledged business kept niggling away at me and for 4 months I listened to the voice in my head,

"Who am I to make a business from this?"
"Would anybody buy one?"

"How can I make them?"

"I have a full time job"

The funny thing with self doubt, is that it likes to protect us, to keep us small and make us feel safe. If you can stand still and acknowledge your doubts and give them a gentle wink and thank them for reminding you that they are there, smile back and calmly say "I will try anyway"

On Saturday October 13th 2012, I officially gave birth to a new a baby and JFTP was born. I had woken up with a thousand thoughts in my head again, I can't quite explain what made me move so quickly, I remember bolting up in bed, feeling completely calm. I grabbed my laptop from my bedside table, flipped open the lid, never one to "properly" shut down my machine just incase I had an inspired moment and posted a poorly photographed picture of Alice's teepee in her bedroom with the words "giveaway" on a facebook page I had created a few weeks prior.

Within 24 hours my new facebook page had acquired 1000 followers, within 1 month it had exceeded 10,000 followers and within a year it would acquire 70,000 followers. It's growth was incredible - and scary! To this day I have never seen another community build with such momentum. I am reminded of the tiny sparks of magic which appear when you are fully aligned with the path you are meant to follow.

It's funny, when you look back and reflect, you can spot the significant imperfect moments creating the next steps on the path ahead.

As my community grew, I had absolutely no idea how to replicate the teepee I had made for Alice, let alone create a business from it. I knew nothing about product testing, patterns or even fabrics. I do however know that had I taken a moment to calm the excitement and stand still to think about all of the things that I didn't know, It is very likely that I wouldn't have gone on to build my company.

The excitement and in some ways, the frenzy created by the community I had accidentally started to build swept me up into a bubble of possibility. It is important to also understand that perception can blind us to the truth. As my platform continued to build and my brand became known worldwide, at it's heart JFTP was still a small business trying to navigate its way through start up and eventually scale up. That can be easy to forget when you have a platform in excess of 100,000 people. Expectations rise and when you throw a national tv program in front of 12 million people into the mix and a famous investor, it felt that I was constantly on a runaway train.

JFTP went on to sell over 100,000 items worldwide, creating millions of magical smiles. It was the pinnacle of entrepreneurial dreams, to build a worldwide brand and scale a company with a product that had such a strong, positive impact.

Throughout my journey I was constantly tested, every test pushing me to my next level as a business owner. As the community started to grow, so did the demand for my teepees. I balanced working full-time in a high pressure environment in a senior role, managing projects with budgets worth millions of pounds. In parallel I was trying to learn how to be a mummy to my little Alice and navigate the early stages of start up, with explosive growth thrown into the mix.

I remember my first sale so clearly, as my online community grew it brought with it an increasing number of product enquiries. The platform reached nearly 2000 followers before my first sale was confirmed. I said yes, accepted a deposit, confirmed the design and then spent a few days wondering how I was going to make another teepee. A week later I had sewn a fully complete teepee which stood tall on 4 6ft poles. Coincidentally my first customer lived a few miles away from me and so I decided to deliver it by hand.

The lady who had purchased the teepee had forgotten to provide me with her new address and so I arrived at the agreed time at her old address. I frantically messaged trying to reach her to confirm the address I should be delivering her teepee to. Eventually she responded and I travelled to Epsom to deliver her teepee. When I arrived she was incredibly agitated, cross with the fact that I was late. She ran out of the door late for a school pick up and asked me to leave the teepee on the doorstep. I was devastated. As my first handmade product, I had worried about it, I had tried to perfect it as much as I possibly could. Anybody who runs a product based company will identify with the feeling that every product you make, includes a little piece of you too.

I left the teepee as requested and drove away, but something kept niggling away at me, the whole situation had been so stressful, did I really want to do this again? My mind monkeys were in full force. 24 hours later I received a very long email from the customer. It detailed every single thing that was wrong with the teepee. The fabric wasn't as expected, it was too tall, the stitching wasn't perfect. Every single element of my beautiful product had been torn apart. I was absolutely devastated. The customers husband returned it back to me the next day. I found it interesting that she had sent her husband rather than face me after the wrath I had just faced from her email. It was the first and last time I provided a refund during those early years.

I could have given up and chosen not to pursue my idea. The lady had validated every doubt I had in my head. She had told me my product wasn't any good, she had told me I couldn't sew, she also told me to stop selling them. She fed every insecurity that I had and as with fears, my self doubt grew and grew until I almost stopped before I had started.

As entrepreneurs we are tested in so many different ways. Business isn't easy, it is as difficult as it is fulfilling and emotionally challenging as it is rewarding. Nobody has the right to ask you to stop pursuing your dreams, listen to the feedback, be thankful for the criticism and take a moment to look internally and explore if there is any truth in what has been shared. Most importantly, do not let the idea that you are unworthy enter your mind, step away from the desire to internalise it and become a victim as a result of somebody else's opinion. Know who you are, commit your dream to yourself and take the next step, no matter how small.

When I stopped and reviewed the feedback the lady had given me, I did see the imperfections. The product wasn't fully ready. I rolled up my sleeves, I recreated the pattern, I found somebody to help me cut the teepee panels, I learnt how to CE test my product, I selected fabrics I could happily work with and I tried again. Within a few months there was a 6 month waiting list for my product and there wasn't a complaint letter in sight.

Over the next 6 years my team grew to 40 seamstresses around the UK, supported by three factories, a large number of freelancers and my very own fabric printing line. I am so incredibly proud of everything the business did achieve and the impact the brand created. It was also a constant shock, given that I didn't know how to sew and my background was in technology.

Last year I was in a fortunate position to mentor a new fashion brand start up. The product was fun and quirky, they were launching into a saturated market, customer expectations were high. They had worked on the product for 2 years before it's launch, perfecting every element of it. It was a wonderful business to be part of. When the product did launch, they sold a few products and I could see that the sales had provided a huge confidence boost.

A few days later when we met, I was expecting them to feel elated, but instead the air felt very grey. They had just received a long email, similar to the email I had received, from a friend they had known for many years who had bought one of their first items. The email was presented as feedback and tore the product apart, calling into question two years of hard work.

I watched them doubt themselves, fall into victim mode and question their friends motives. The feedback had been taken to heart in the worst possible way. Why? because it came from a friend, somebody they thought they could trust, somebody they had shared life experiences with. Eventually they were able to find the good within the feedback and used it to move forward with.

Those closest to us can often be the first to cast a stone, some will want to protect you, others will worry and a few may reflect the failure of pursing their dreams onto you. Very much like I had to and as did my mentees, accept the feedback, be thankful for it. There may even be a degree of truth hidden amongst the words, use the feedback to move forward with and continue building your business. Handing over your dreams to somebody else to decide if they are worthy or not, should never be an option.

There are many many stories I can share which happened over the years, I have so many incredible learnings and whilst this book is very much around my personal journey with my business, I do also want those of you who have an idea to start a business or are even midst a business journey to also take away something from my story. I believe full heartedly that building a business is a gift, it's your opportunity to imagine a better future and create a lasting impact with your work. However it is as much about the person as it is about the business. Knowing who you are, your values and building a network of support around you will help you to stand tall against the most challenging of battles.

Chapter 3: The Heroes Journey

"If the path before you is clear, you are probably on someone else's"

Joseph Campbell

Dragons Den has formed a huge part of my story, it is often the area of my story which people tend to ask me about first. I wanted to share my experience with you, in the hope that if you are considering it for your business, you will have a fully rounded picture of the experience, rather than the edited version you see on TV. Ultimately I would love for you to make a decision that feels right for you.

Since 4th January 2005, Dragons Den has aired across our TV screens, viewers are drawn in to the show, by the entrepreneurs, the stories, the businesses and the pitches - the good and the bad! As a nation, we have supported the show for 15 years, watched many different types of entrepreneurs walk into the den and face the dragons and pitch their businesses.

I still remember the early years when business owners like Rob Law entered the Den in 2006 with his product - Trunki. For those of you who may not be familiar with Trunki, it is a children's travel brand, which includes amazing travel suitcases, which children can ride on. Rob's success didn't come from the den as he didn't receive investment, despite the wonderful product and the brilliant pitch. Funnily enough Trunki is dubbed as one of Dragons Den's most famous rejections. Dragons Den became a small part of his story as he went on to build a global brand.

There were so many other businesses too, Simon Booth entered the Den in 2011 with his business, Kiddimoto. He didn't secure investment, but went on to build a global company which celebrated it's 16th year in business this year and then there was the tangle teezer, where Shaun Pulfrey failed to grab the attention of the dragons in 2007, the business is now dubbed as the £200 million Dragons Den reject.

Whilst there are many many examples, these were the few that stood out for me. They didn't need the support and investment from the dragons to go on and build amazing, successful companies. They had the drive and passion to formulate their own paths and pave the way to success. It does also go to show, that the dragons, despite their phenomenal experience and savvy approach to business, can also miss an opportunity.

Personally, Dragons Den fascinated me. I was never really interested in the dragons themselves, I wasn't a fan of the tactics they used, it made me feel uncomfortable watching the dragons strip people down so publicly on national tv, even if that was it's raison d'etre. Ramifications for public humiliation can be devastating, especially as you have no control over the edits and the first time you see the episode is alongside millions of people nationwide, there is little room to prepare. What attracted me were the business owners, they were so passionate about their products, they believed full heartedly in their businesses. You could see the excitement amongst the pitches, the stories they shared and those all important numbers.

When I set out to build JFTP, I didn't have any aspirations to bring my business in front of the dragons. The negative side of the program pushed the desire to enter the show to the back of my mind.

What if they didn't like the business?

What if the numbers didn't stack up?

What if the product failed in front of millions of people?

What if they said no?

Could the brand survive?

Would it hurt everything I had worked so hard to build?

Speaking to lots of other Dragons Den contestants, they share the same sentiments. It takes a lot of courage to push through the "what if's" and show up for your business in such a public way.

I can't quite explain why I did fill out the BBC application on the website in December 2013. A few members of my community had mentioned it in passing and I had made a few jokes about it on my platform. One Sunday evening, out of impulse, I just decided to fill out the application. I didn't check the application a million times, I didn't give myself any time to think about it. I literally filled out the application in front of me, hit submit and then forgot about it until I received a phone call from a BBC researcher in early January, as I walked through Waterloo Station on my way home from my full time job in London.

I spoke to a really lovely lady who asked me questions about my business and my application. At this point I was crouched down into a little ball underneath the stairwell at the end
of Waterloo Station trying to listen to her. The conversation ended with an invite to the
BBC studios. The aim was to practice a pitch on camera which would be shared with the
director and his / her team, they would then assess the business, the product and me to
see if I was a good fit. In parallel I was also asked to send in a business plan, a profit and
loss forecast and my product testing certificates.

As a new business owner who had formed her company based on a pattern, created with
26 sheets of A4 plain paper cello taped together and started spontaneously one Saturday
morning, it is safe to assume I didn't have a business plan. I also had no idea what a profit
and loss forecast was. I did however have my product testing certificates - phew! Que the
cramming and the learning and working with my accountant to pull everything together to
not only create the needed paperwork, but to also formulate the business as a Ltd company and apply for a trademark to protect the brand. This was the moment when JFTP started to feel like a real business as opposed to the side business I was building alongside my
full time job.

I explored every aspect of my company and how I wanted it to unfold. Over the years I
learnt that the key was to ensure you reviewed the forecasts on a monthly basis, it became
my guiding light. As the business grew and the numbers started to get bigger and bigger,
my forecasts would help me to anticipate if and when I needed a cash injection, often

during a quieter period. I knew the cost of my items, which drove my pricing and the salaries I could pay my team.

I understood if I could afford to move into the bigger office, when we needed more space. They were fundamental in helping me to drive my monthly revenue targets. I was able to make decisions based on the facts in front of me. My investor once told me that "your numbers will tell a story" she was right! I know how to look at a set of accounts, a cash flow and P&L forecasts and understand how a business is 'actually' operating. It is something I undertake meticulously every month with all of my companies and I would advise all business owners, no matter how small your business is to establish the same cadence.

I really enjoyed this process, it helped me to stand still and think about the aspirations I had for my company and the goals I wanted to achieve. The business plan helped to shape the way the business operated. The Profit and Loss forecast also drove a cashflow forecast, which not only helped me to understand my costs in detail, but the money I needed to have in my bank account to ensure that the business could continue to grow and build momentum.

Dragons Den helped to shape me as a business owner. As I went through the process I grew in confidence, guided clearly by the path laying out in front of me, I felt myself transition into a CEO, cemented by the fact that I took a leap of faith and left my full time job in London following the filming for the show.

The "test" filming in London in early February was a lot of fun. I travelled by Taxi with several teepees in hand. Carrying 6 ft long teepees around London would have been a fun challenge, however I chose to approach the day with as little stress as possible. I practiced my pitch, introducing myself and my business over and over again until I could stand confidently in front of the camera.

Cameras are a funny thing! I notice it with Alice. If she is ever on video with her friends, her little voice changes, I watch on thinking "that's not how she speaks" it turns out I did exactly the same thing. I used so many different pitch levels, pronounced my words in ways I would never normally, until eventually I settled and it was just me. I believe that was the edit they used in the end. Authenticity always wins.

The wait was quite short and a few weeks later I found out I would be filming at the BBC studios in Manchester in mid March. I wasn't ready! I panicked, my thoughts started running wild in my head. I had 3 stone to lose, perfect products to create, write a winning pitch and memorise it, whilst running my company and holding down my full time job. The reality is, I was fine just as I was. I had the perfect product, as I had already shown up with them, alongside the happy customers we were already making the teepees for and I knew my pitch as I had been working on it for a few weeks, how I looked, well lets just say when I popped my dress on and my favourite royal purple suede shoes, I was more than happy with how I would show up as.

My wonderful neighbour Cat came to sit with me in my office one night and worked through the pitch with me, we discussed the options of going on the show and not going on the show. Cat lived next door to me and is one of the smartest women I know and incredibly kind, she is definitely one of my favourite humans. Not to mention super mum to 3 children, holding down a part time job, running a company called Totally Mama and representing Great Britain in the Triathlon in her age category!

I just felt so nervous, I didn't want to damage my business in anyway. I knew it's growth was special and the brand was gaining incredible momentum. Cat's objectivity and willingness to listen helped me to jump over the hurdle I had created for myself. Whilst the nerves still sat in my tummy, I knew this was a great way to show up for my business and showcase it to the world. "Small steps' became my go to and even now as I build my companies, "small steps" is prevalent in everything I do. I was looking ahead and fearing the whole piece, when in reality all I had to do was take the next logical step and see where it would take me. It's also really helpful to reach out to a friend, family member or mentor to gain a little perspective, we often trap ourselves inside our heads, a different outlook can only ever help.

During Mid March 2014, I travelled up to Manchester, with my teepees and accessories in hand and with Angela, my mother in law for moral support. I had memorised my pitch, the teepees and accessories looked really lovely and I felt ready. Truth be told I had no idea what the experience would hold, other than QVC, a few years earlier, I had never been on TV before. When we arrived in Manchester I went straight to the studios to set up my teepees and accessories for an early morning inspection by the director and his team. They could still decide not to proceed, in fact up until the moment you are called into the studio to film, you could be sent home. Passing the product inspection or sitting in the green room (which was literally green) didn't guarantee you a slot.

I do remember feeling incredibly nervous that night. Nobody, apart from close friends and family knew I was filming to appear on Dragons Den. The next day I found myself at the studio at 7am for the inspection. The director placed his arm around me, gave me a gentle cuddle and with the words "You have done quite well haven't you" lit me up from the inside. I had passed the first stage. As was quite common with JFTP, it created this bubble of high energy and happiness for anybody who stepped towards it. By the end of the show I had sold products to crew, makeup and even another contestant. JFTP never ceased to amaze me.

Filming was a long day. We started early, following the product inspection, we each had to film entering the lift, getting out of the lift, meeting hair-and-make-up, making friends with the 'runners' and the other business owners. The wait in the green room meant we could practice our pitch. I did also ring my accountant to check on a few details, to then find a runner standing in front of me asking me what I was doing. We weren't allowed to make phone calls. One little white lie later I was off the hook.

Around lunchtime, as I was waiting for my sandwich, I was told to go into hair-and-makeup for a touch up as I was due to go into the Den to deliver my pitch. Panic started to set in - I was hungry and they wanted me to go into the Den... now! I am notorious for getting hangry, it has followed me around my whole life. Here I was about to go into the Den, to possibly get eaten alive by 5 incredibly savvy business people and there was a strong possibility that hangry me would walk in instead!

As we approached the recording studio, we walked down a long corridor, I could hear the the words from the walkie talkies from the runner who was walking next to me. The Dragons were on the move from their dressing rooms. The next thing I knew I had 4 runners surrounding me, blocking my view. I wasn't allowed to see or meet any of the Dragons prior to filming, when they passed and we. were safely inside the studio, I was able to continue walking forward.

I was in the Den for over two hours answering the questions constantly thrown at me by Deborah Meaden, Peter Jones, Piers Linney, Kelly Hoffen and Duncan Ballentyne. I just kept on bouncing back with a reply. It was the one time in my life where I was thankful for 'having an answer for everything'. There is much to be said about what happened inside the Den. It was an eye-opener and TV at its best. When the show finally aired on August 24th, 2014, there is a clip of Peter asking me to climb inside a teepee in heels to show him the size of the teepee, disbelieving that an adult could fit inside. This was the one part of the entire show I had worried about constantly during the gap between filming and when the episode aired. I prayed and hoped that I hadn't managed to flash my knickers on National TV. I had no idea how much grace I had managed to get in and out of the teepee with in my dress and my beautiful purple shoes.

Throughout my pitch, offers came in from Duncan, Kelly and Deborah. I had requested £50,000 for 20% of my business. In the end I chose Deborah and gave away 25%. Lots and lots of people have asked me over the years, why I made that decision, when Kelly would have been more suitable, as well as wanting less equity. To be honest a few things happened, whilst I was standing on that yellow spot, marked on the floor for the camera's. My instincts kept screaming Deborah at me over and over again. I also had no concept what 20% or 25% really meant. You can agree to 50% if you feel that the investor is worth bringing onboard and will contribute the knowledge needed to get you to where you want to be. But 50% of nothing isn't a great deal anyway and without them you will never really know what is possible.

I often ask myself, even to this day, why I chose Deborah. I always arrive back to the same answer. I was instinctively navigated towards choosing her. Had I chosen Kelly maybe things would have turned out differently, but I genuinely believe that we are all here to help each other on our journeys. For whatever reason - and perhaps only the universe knew - Deborah turned up on my path. The lessons I learnt over the next few years changed the person I was, how I led my company and how I viewed the world. I think Deborah became a part of my world to shape me into a business owner, to toughen me up and to help me to believe in my own ability. The path was set and onward I bound.

Chapter 4: The space in between

"Find a place inside where there's joy, and the joy will burn out the pain"
Joseph Campbell

There is much to be said about the three years that followed Dragons Den. The lessons hiding within the journey strengthened my resolve and helped me to build the resilience I needed to run my company. It became so important to me to surround myself with people that I trusted and whilst many would advise not to work with family, I leaned into mine and welcomed my mum and mother in law into the business to help me look after customer care.

Clive stepped in to become a director in the company, looking after all things operational. The team gave him a gift when we moved to our new office in 2016, his very own sign, perfectly balanced on the door "Welcome to my man cave." He carved out a space for himself within a female dominated company, bringing bouts of dry humour which often had everybody rolling on the floor, accompanied by an eye roll from me.

Working with my husband was definitely something we both had to get used to. It was important to us both to carve out areas which we owned and whilst JFTP was my company and all decisions fell to me, I never needed to ask about dispatch or stock ordering, Clive took care of it. We somehow found a balance, respected each others space and whilst the long working hours would fall to me, it was comforting to know that he was there.

Surrounding myself with people I could trust was a response to the exposure I felt. Since Dragons Den had aired, I opened both myself and the business up to a level of expectation I hadn't anticipated. From the fiery messages I would receive at the lack of boys prints and shock at my lack of focus on gender neutral items, to the way I ran the company. It often caused me to scratch my head. As the sticks continued to be thrown I couldn't help but take it personally.

Trust in business is a virtue many have fallen fowl to over the years. There are so many stories regarding sour business relationships, theft from team members, loss of financial income as a result of a bad decisions. These stories create fear and cause us to be wary of what we are stepping into. Whilst awareness is a blessing, be mindful of pre-framing your story with fear before it even begins. I have always been a little naive, I like to see the best in people as a starting point and I give trust easily. I believe with my whole heart that trust is a key foundation to build your business upon. Without it you will nurture a resentful culture, which will thrive on fear and drive bad decisions.

I will admit after dragons den, the exposure to having showcased my business on national tv, rocked the safe world I had built. I was overwhelmed with the holes that people chose to pick in my business. Where there weren't any complaints previously, we were suddenly facing people wanting compensation for having to wait for their items a little longer than normal. Dragons Den heightened the greed and I also think as a result of the association with my famous investor, it was somehow assumed that we had access to her wealth. I did experience theft from members of my team, I did experience the fallout of badly timed business decisions and at the end of 2014, I almost lost the company I had built as a result of making a decision to follow guidance, my intuition had screamed at me not to follow.

I began to lose sight of who I was and what I wanted for my business. If I look back now and reflect, I can see those moments where I veered off course onto a path that didn't feel right for me. It is a stark lesson and reminds me that the guidance system we hold within us is paramount. Listen to it! It knows who you are and the path which is right for you. It is the very reason it is there.

It was during this period that I experienced my first contact with a deliberately formed on-line 'hate group', set up on social media to belittle me personally and essentially bring the company I had built to it's knees. The group would advise people to obtain a refund if they had purchased from us and to buy from new competitors who were now popping up around us. These tactics played hard on our cash flow and often distracted me from running the business and building out the team to deal with the explosive growth we were experiencing.

It was strange to me that somebody would spend the time they had been gifted on this earth deliberately causing upset to another, I still believe to this day, that the lady who had created this group felt that she needed a space for her voice to be heard. I genuinely couldn't understand it. In reality the lady who had founded the group was unhappy with the teepee she had bought from us, she didn't make any attempts to reach out or to return it, instead she chose to build platform which worked hard every single day to disparage what I was building. Over the years I did reach out to her, we tried to find an amicable way through her grievances, however her dislike was so intense she refused to allow me to re-solve what had happened.

On February 24th 2015 I finally threw in the towel, feeling trapped and backed into a cor-ner. Every time we had tried to move ahead with the business, she counteracted with neg-ative reviews on trustpilot. I found myself in a dance with somebody I had never met be-fore, pushing good reviews onto trustpilot to drown out the bad, to then find another bar-rage for negative reviews. The team at trustpilot understood what was happening and they tried to stop them from posting by blocking their IP Addresses. However given that their IP addresses weren't static, their attempts were futile.

In the end I surrendered and what I now recognise to be in alignment with the universe, I stopped fighting and just like that my resistance fell away. I genuinely believe in my heart that we have the power to change our point of attraction at any moment, this event showed me the enormous power you can gain over yourself when you step forward and own something, rather than try to battle it in the dark by yourself. I posted a long post on my page, apologising, explaining and eventually surrendering. I closed down my laptop and walked away. I was tired.

Clive and I then took Alice to school and on a sombre drive we drove to our offices in Dork-ing. I wasn't sure what would happen next, I did however recognise the huge relief I felt. Somehow the weight of the last 6 months had lifted and what would come, would come. When I reached the office, my team were waiting for me. A. few people looked worried and then Emma spoke "Have you seen your facebook page?"

In response to the post I had shared, explaining the past 6 months, the platform did what it always did best. It folded in to support me and the business. People began sharing amazing comments of support, flowers arrived and a positive group to show support to the business was set up. I do also want to stress that messages of these types do need to be worded with care. People did also choose to jump over to the group and berate the lady who had created it, this wasn't something that I advocated or wanted to happen. However we all behave in ways that we feel is best at the time and I understood the sentiments. By the end of the day, the group I had tormented myself over for almost 180 days closed.

As delighted as I was, social media had shown her power, her ability to jump from support to hate in an instant. I knew that I had survived as a result of the support from the community I had built, I vowed not to take it for granted. But I was wary and without realising it, I started to distance myself. I limited the personal posts and focussed on the company. In retrospect I was protecting myself, my family and my business. The glimpse I had into a world full of exposure following Dragons Den frightened me. It isn't a surprise to learn that the day I decided to voluntarily liquidate my wonderful business unearthed this period from within me, it was deep rooted in fear and as is common with fear, it raises it's ugly head and grows bigger and bigger as you feed it with more thoughts and energy. However what fear wasn't prepared for was at the point I made the decision to voluntarily liquidate my business I chose that day to lead with love and as we all, love trumps fear, every single time.

As the months rolled by, I started to notice a change in my behaviour and temperament. My bubbly personality, which I am known for started to mutate into a grey cloud. I was trying my best to lead the company through explosive growth, with very little support. Attempting to make decisions which would protect the brand I had built, yet at every stage a little piece of who I was and all of the reasons I started my business began to get chipped away at. At the time, I hadn't spotted the signs that I was disconnecting and folding into myself. The happiness I once felt when I created a new teepee, started to feel like a burden, the responsibilities of holding down and leading an ever growing team and the request to fulfil my shareholder commitments weighed heavy around my neck. At the time I assumed it was normal to feel this way, that these were the responsibilities of a business owner growing towards the elusive million pound mark. I couldn't have been more wrong.

I am mindful of narrating the three years that followed. There are parts of the journey I am happy to keep to myself, content with knowing the truth, without the need to justify parts of the JFTP story. The business did go on to achieve great things and whilst I did get a lot of things wrong, I never ever once stopped trying to do the right thing.

My heart swells with pride when I think back to the thousands and thousands of teepees we sent out to homes across the world. I still remember the 1000's of photos we were sent every week, of tiny people with their happy little faces looking back at me, full of excitement and adventure. I am proud of the fact that we built a team of 40 seamstresses across the UK who supported our production, whilst providing the opportunity to flexibly work around their families, alongside our factories and suppliers. I smile at the yearly events we held at our offices, often with ques from our incredible customers who showed up to support us. I love the fact that we raised in excess of £20,000 for the right to play charity by giving away one of our hidden hole products or that #JFTPMagic trended on twitter during the Ruby Worldcup. It's staggering to think back to 2016 when I launched the franchise arm of my company, attracting 10,000 applications within a 2 week period just by posting the information on our Facebook platform, or that we went on to lead the way with handmade and scale it in a way that had never been seen before and I am so proud to know that when I look out on the horizon in front of me at the many many handmade businesses now creating their own paths, I can occasionally spot glimpses of the business that I loved.

The business never ever ceased to amaze me, it still does. The value in JFTP was never monetary, the power of the brand far outweighed the monetary value of the business. The feeling JFTP would invoke when our products would arrive in a new home, the giggle you could hear from inside our teepees. It was the love and kindness every single one of our items was made with, which then took on a lease of life of its own as they entered their new home. JFTP encapsulated the magic for all children across the world, whilst subtly fighting for every child to have the right to have a safe place for play and to have the ability to dream and imagine. My wonderful business went on to surpass every possible expectation I could have for it. I will forever be grateful for the gift I had been given to bring it to life and for the incredible journey it took me on. It will always hold a very special place in my soul and whilst I know I will go on to build other companies, I recognise that there was something very special about Just For Tiny People.

Chapter 5: Breaking your Heart to Heal Your Soul

"The cave you fear to enter, holds the treasure you seek"

Joseph Campbell

I came across a quote one day on my instagram feed

"Sometimes you have to break your heart in order to heal your soul"

It stopped me in my tracks, the words resonated with me so deeply, I felt that they had somehow found their way to show themselves just for me, in that moment, a total sum of the past 18 months.

I am a huge believer in fate and the ways of the universe. I have come to believe that co-incidence is just perfect alignment. I also believe wholeheartedly that we are here on this earth to evolve as human beings and ensure our soul experiences everything it needs to in order to complete its journey in this lifetime. Our life is a contract with our soul, our intuition is the guidance system that enables us to navigate through life and our thoughts create our beliefs, which in turn create the reality that we live everyday.

When I first saw this quote, the words fell off the screen. I remember just sitting there and feeling a huge wave of relief. It made such sense to me. The breaking of my heart to make a decision which not only closed the business I loved and changed the way we lived our life, took me on a journey which tested everything that I knew and eventually healed my soul. When you have nothing, not a penny to your name, there is nowhere left to hide within yourself, even good feelings of thought, we are encouraged to reach for, seem out of reach. During those quiet days, it's just you and you, forced to look at who you are and everything that you stand for.

The moments when I felt brave enough to look at the person staring back at me, I found it difficult to comprehend who I was, especially internally. I was materialistic, I placed work and commitment before love, my relationship and my family. I chose money as an exchange for my time and friendships and I measured my worth by the success I had accumulated over the years.

I remember when I was a little girl, we were all sitting around the dinner table, chatting and eating. With 3 other siblings, it was a pretty noisy household, midst the noise, I clearly remember my mum telling my dad that his "heart was falling out of his pocket" I saw him take his hand and put it straight on the pocket of his short sleeved shirt. Inside the pocket, he kept his money, always close by, protected. It now makes me smile that I can see this memory so clearly and understand the impact it had on me. The foundations we lay for our children, are through not only the words that we speak, but by the actions that we take.

It was no surprise to me that I placed money ahead of everything and everyone I loved, including how I regarded myself.

I no longer experienced joy, or knew how to laugh, the genuine kind, which comes from your soul. Sure, I knew how to smile at the right times and to say the right things, but if you had taken a closer look, the light had disappeared from behind my eyes. Everything I thought I was and held as important no longer existed in my life, I had stripped myself bare.

The universe had delivered its ultimate blow and without a roof over our heads I realised that in order to move forward and rebuild my life, I had to find me again, who I was, what I liked and didn't like, what I valued and where I felt most at peace. I wanted to feel the love that surrounded me and laugh until my belly hurt. I wanted to stand still and listen to the sound of the birds and find joy in the world around me. But first I had to find a way to live in a world where I had felt such loss.

The dark nights had shown me loneliness and exclusion, it had shown me the rawness of the pain and guilt I had felt and in doing so, it also reminded me to look for the stars. They held the light that would move me forwards. At night I clung to the stars, sometimes wishing on them as I had when I was a little girl. At the time, I hadn't realised that I had started to look for a better feeling thought, something to improve the way I was feeling and more importantly to change the thoughts that were consuming me.

When you feel your heart breaking your instinct is to wrap yourself up in an armour of denial to try and protect yourself from feeling any form of pain. There is brutality in thinking that you have to find the strength to brush it under the rug and move forward. Pain has a way of following you around, it attaches itself to you, a little like the sticky green plant we all used to throw at each other when we were little. The only way to clear the pain is to face it. Facing something that has hurt you, isn't pretty. It's hard and ugly, it's filled with self doubt and tears and every now and then a bout of anxiety you can't shift. The release comes when you realise that the story you are telling yourself has changed, it no longer owns you, instead you own it. We are built to deal with hard things, no matter what anybody says. We are loving and resilient and kind and we have everything we need inside of us to heal, gather strength and go again.

If you can, be aware that past thoughts and memories like to pop up and remind you every now and then that they are still there. The reality is they won't permanently leave you. Every memory you have and every action you have ever taken forms a part of who you are. As they say we are a "sum of all parts" but if you allow your past, your mistakes and anything that you view as "bad" prevent you from showing up in the world as your real self, you will deny yourself the opportunity to live the life that you want for yourself.

The decision to close down JFTP was one of the hardest decisions I have ever had to make. Any business owner will tell you that your business is very much like your child. During the early years, there is much excitement as you nurture your vision and bring it to life. As it starts to grow, very much like a teenager, your business will argue with you, challenge you and cause you to question the decisions you have made. The sleepless nights are many, masked by the pretence that all is well, the journey is often lonely and the pressure to make the right decisions is incredibly stressful.

Somehow though, at the end of the day, the pride you have in yourself for having built something extraordinary, positively impacting people around the world is indescribable. Which is why closing or even selling a company will always be one of the toughest, emotionally challenging decisions you will ever have to make. All stories have an ending, how yours ends is sometimes taken out of your hands, but choosing to do the right thing, at the right time, will always be a decision that only you can ever make.

Following the airing of Dragons Den in 2014, JFTP had been catapulted into a period of extraordinary growth. The pace to produce our products, to hire additional team members to cope with the demand and to remain on-top of cash flow, whilst making hundreds of decisions was in truth, something I was unprepared for. As a person I am very creative, I am also very lucky to be a stickler for organisation, I know how to manage big teams and maintain delivery momentum, whilst achieving huge goals. I love gaining traction and moving at pace, if you ask anybody who has worked with me, my favourite word has always been "momentum." Handling the aftermath of Dragons Den should have been manageable for me. I had trained for 15 years in the corporate world, for moments like this. The skills I had acquired should have equipped me to deal with everything that was happening, at the pace it was happening at.

Yet somehow it had knocked me off my feet. The reality was, I had allowed people to knock me off my feet. The designer who had created my first logo and a number of assets for my products issued me with legal papers out of the blue claiming copyright, wanting to sue me. The production team I had formed to help us cope with demand, decided to increase costs, which weren't planned for, effecting both cash flow and our product margins. New members of the customer care team were needing to be onboarded quickly, to help cope with the increase in messages we were receiving, without the correct systems in place. The website kept falling over and needed to be moved from a shared to a managed platform. National TV had escalated everything, the business had moved from a start up to scale up in a matter of weeks. In hindsight, these incidents taught me the need for copyright and production contracts and why they are so important within business, providing a safety net which enables you to operate within. But more importantly it showed a side of humanity that I just couldn't understand and in truth it hurt me deeply.

My husband, Clive will often tell me that I am naive, he airs on the side of pessimism. If I tell him about a piece of good news, he will always, without fail rebuff it. I know exactly what he will say. I have learnt over the years, to laugh it off, smile and just allow him to say what he needs to. In a lot of ways it's great fun living with somebody who challenges my view of the world. I will however always protect what I believe - with every ounce of my being. I respect his view and in turn he respects mine.

If being naive, looks for the good in people and expects empathy and kindness towards each other, I am more than happy to be naive. I just don't know how else to be. I won't ever stop believing in the good of people.

On August 16th 2017, I made the very hard decision to close down the company I loved and step away. It followed a live event we had hosted on our Facebook platform the night before, the entire concept had been branded as "JFTP TV". Every day of the week we were hosting Live events, showcasing our products, sometimes there were in excess of 10,000 people watching. It was amazing. From the outside, the business was successful, everything looked exactly as it should.

This particular night was different though, my little Alice had been showing off a few of our products. She would often ask to host a live event, occasionally I wouldn't mind and would hand her my phone to host the live event from.

I was so proud of the confidence she was showing, she was 6 years old chatting away to 10,000 people online. As she chatted away she started to read the comments that were coming through, people choosing that very moment to abuse me, call me names, swear at me, suggest I was running a scam. The following events happened so very quickly. I can't explain why, after 7 years, in that moment I literally snapped. Something broke inside of me. I stepped outside of my body and peered in and felt such a clear realisation that no matter what opinions others may have, I no longer wanted to be a punching bag for other peoples bad decisions and more importantly there was absolutely no way I would place Alice in a position where she would have to witness or be privy to this type of behaviour.

Over the years, following Dragons Den, as a result of the increased exposure, I had removed photos of her from popular mum based websites, where a few people had made the decision to use her photo to berate me or my products. I had to call in the police when death threats were received. I accepted the online abuse over and over, I "thought" it was part and parcel of the level of success the business was experiencing. I thought that this was normal, to live my life so openly, leaving every choice I made open to criticism by people who had never built a business or didn't have the experience to know anymore than I did. I knew it didn't feel normal, it didn't feel like something that should be happening.

For 6 years I allowed it. I allowed it into my world, never once defending myself or correcting misinformed information. You are damned if you do and you are damned if you don't and on a platform which reached 7 million people a week, I thought there was no place for my truth. But that night, for the first time ever I saw, in a blink of an eye, the damaging effect this abuse could have on the person who is the most precious to me. My Alice.

I chose to protect her. There is no other reason. I closed the business I loved, to protect the incredible human I was raising. Alice deserves to live in a world of magic, to believe in the good in people, she deserves to be unknown and to live her life as she chooses, to make mistakes without the world watching her. And so in that moment, when I broke, I made a decision that would eventually heal us all.

Alice is now 9, though sometimes I think she is going on 17. She is incredibly independent, loves to sleep in and acutely aware of everything that goes on around her. She is also a very smart, kind, little girl, with a wonderful love for learning. Over the years we have discussed what happened with JFTP and that there are unkind things about me online. I have always been really honest with her and have done my best to explain. She accepted what I shared and we have all found a way to move on. Every now and then she will retell a memory of something good that happened when I ran JFTP, she remembers the events, the market nights and the time we all spent at the office, creating and making.

For years she hasn't mentioned that night, yet the other day she pulled me aside and told me that she had googled my name as she had wanted to find a picture of me. She quietly whispered to me "mummy you are still famous."

The reality is, she is growing up and there will be things I cannot protect her from. Her curiosity will lead her to so many places. Do I want her to read that somebody thought it would be appropriate to call her mummy a scam artist online, of course not. Do I want her to see the joy people took in sharing our home online when it first went on the market and the derogatory things that were said, or the open group that somebody so cruelly left open to deliberately taunt me - no absolutely not.

However they are there and they form part of what has been. And so if she has questions, we talk about them. I use it as an opportunity to explain that Social Media can sometimes be hurtful and unkind and people will write things if they feel unheard or are having a difficult time and when they feel better, they are so busy being happy, they will forget the comments they have made and take them down. In the same breath I show her The Kindness Company, which I now own and show her that there is still very much good in the world.

Ahead of that fateful evening, there had been whisperings that I would choose to close my company, many wished that I would. It wasn't something that I wanted. The business had racked up a lot of debt to maintain the production level we were operating at, outside support was elusive and I felt that I was caught underneath a mound I had no idea how to dig myself out of. The reality is, the problem was no worse than the situation I had recovered from during 2014, following Dragons Den, where we had over traded and I had to rebuild the business.

The difference this time was me. I had lost all faith, I no longer had the passion that I had for this magical business I had created. Every ounce of me was exhausted. I could see the impact the business was having on everybody around me, including me team and the people I loved. I just wanted to step away.

The steps that followed weren't my finest hour. As soon as I saw the messages streaming through onto the phone that Alice was holding, my team started to ping me, begging me to get offline. But no, I was angry, I stood tall and faced off against the hate mob, I swore, up setting a mum with her young child watching the live event, (which I still feel incredibly sad about) I screamed and yelled and goaded them to come and find me, to stand in front of me and look me in the eye and repeat what they had written. It was awful, I had become exactly what they wanted to me become - weak and angry and in all honesty I felt it.

It is incredibly easy to sit outside and be a spectator to something unfolding in front of you, to take "facts" and morph them into a story. I remember the following day so clearly, I hadn't slept and after laying awake the entire night thinking about the business and how we had arrived here, I surprisingly felt so incredibly calm the next morning.

I looked at my husband who was physically and emotionally exhausted from the past few months and I wanted nothing more than to see him smile again. He told me quite honestly that the hate was far worse than the cancer battle he had faced years earlier. Retelling that to another human is difficult, as most will assume that we are underestimating the depths of what cancer means. We know exactly what it means having lost loved ones to this awful disease and everything we went through to heal my amazing hubs.

It was in that moment that I realised I had to break my heart. I knew the decision I had to make and without any emotion, I picked up the phone and called the liquidators and asked them to place my wonderful company into voluntary liquidation.

I made the decision to close down JFTP because it was the right thing to do, without further thought as to what might come next or how we would pay our financial commitments. I knew deep down that everything would change, the life we had lived would morph into another season and so I began the journey to say goodbye.

I underestimated what that journey would mean and how reconnecting with your soul would force you to question and explore areas of your life you had hidden from. I also underestimated the impact it would have on everybody around us, but I knew if we had kept going the impact to our little girl and to ourselves, would have been far worse.

Many, many people have contacted me over the years to ask why I didn't issue a public apology, they assumed I had waltzed away into the sunset, without a care in the world. That assumption couldn't be further from the truth.

As soon as I had placed JFTP into liquidation, I got to work. I handed the keys to the liquidators, along with the order book, the bank accounts and paypal accounts. I handed over the stock we had made, which had been safely stored at the fulfilment company.

Many of our orders were paid via payment plans. Upon receipt of the second payment, we always made the items within the order. The order would normally be released upon receipt of the 3rd or 4th payment. Everything was there, being held at the fulfilment centre. I asked over and over what would happen to the outstanding orders, I was assured that if the stock could be retrieved, the orders would be fulfilled.

I soon learnt that Liquidation is a tricky period, regulated with a number of rules and laws that have to be followed. As soon as the business is handed over, everything and everybody closes in. The liquidators were overwhelmed with the volume of calls they were receiving, all goaded by groups set up online to advise people on how to get their money back, by people who weren't informed correctly and unfamiliar with the process.

In reality it just made everything worse. If everybody had been allowed to do their job and provide the process with the time to work, all of our customers would have received their orders. Unfortunately that didn't happen.

I genuinely understood the anger and the number of questions which were flooding in. The rumours had whipped up a frenzy, messages were pouring in and our customers wanted answers. It was frustrating to watch everything unfold, unable to comment or say anything.

With much sadness I watched as groups were set up to support people, often providing incorrect information, adding more fuel to the fire. I watched the JFTP sewing team offer their services to make uncertified products for others. I watched people comment on my ability to run a company over and over and share every piece of information about me all over the internet.

I am so incredibly grateful to the haters who followed me around online for years. Why? because in doing so I was forced to make a decision to stop, reset and look deeply at the person I had become. I discovered not only my purpose and my values, I also have the greatest joy in showing back up in the world as genuinely me.

Many people over the years have contacted me to ask why I didn't say anything following the closure. Technically I wasn't able to. When a business is handed over to a liquidation firm, they take control of the business and have to handle the communication, alongside a number of strict rules. Legally the business owner is unable to, they cannot show preferential treatment to anybody who could be deemed as a creditor, if they do, they risk going to prison.

Had I been able to post an explanation, the truth is at first, I didn't know what to say. I was angry. Angry at everybody. All those who had jumped on the bandwagon when we were riding the wave of success, yet stepped away without a word when things started to get a little tough and I was angry at myself for making the decision to close my wonderful company. Much time has now passed and anger, as it always does, finds a way of passing. I have chosen to view the events in a way that enables me to accept what has happened for the sake of the journey I have been on.

My only wish is that I could have said good bye. I would have loved the opportunity to reflect on 6 amazing years, to thank my team, suppliers and most importantly my customers. It would have been nice to have had the opportunity to reflect on the journey and acknowledge all those who had believed in the business from the very moment I launched it. I would have thanked Dragons Den for showcasing JFTP to the world and empowering so many people to welcome magic into their world. I would have smiled at the many businesses who followed, who have created a space with their businesses, inspired by JFTP, some, now completely unaware. It was my absolute pleasure to have built a business, whose legacy still exists in thousands of homes around the world.

I would have also liked the opportunity to say sorry, to all those who had supported the business who felt let down by the decision I made. I would have explained that my decision was never intended to create upset or leave anybody without and I would have explained the plan I had tried to put in place to ensure everybody would have been looked after.

I would have explained that sometimes stories have to end, sometimes in ways you would never have expected, yet also encouraged you to build what is in your heart, to take the next step forward to start your journey, which would help you to leave a mark on the world.

Building a business takes an awful lot of courage and sacrifice, there are decisions that are made behind the scenes which nobody will ever know about. There are many many directors I know who have placed the security of their home on the line to raise finance for a business they believe in. Business is a lifestyle, a show up every day and commit, even on the days when the sun is hidden behind the clouds, type of lifestyle.

Business also has the capacity to change the world, entrepreneurs can make a real difference by putting their best foot forward and build a legacy through the businesses they create. It is a world I adore and will always adore as it is so closely linked to my purpose. I fundamentally believe that we all have it within ourselves to create a business and change the world. I also believe that the only limitations we face are those that we place on ourselves. But first you have to change your narrative, you have to explore your story and accept the journey you have been on and guard the life experiences you have gained along the way as precious gems. These are your gifts to the world, gifts that only you can share.

The journey has been 8 years long and finally my soul has found peace and happiness. it knows laughter, love and gratitude, in a place I am so happy to call home, surrounded by people I am incredibly lucky to call friends and family.

Sometimes the only path you can follow is the very next step.

Chapter 6: Slaying Inner Dragons

"The black moment is the moment when the real message of transformation is going to come. At the darkest moment comes the light"

Joseph Campbell

During the past few years I have often wondered how I would find my way back. I knew from the moment I handed back the keys to JFTP that I would run another company. I tried so incredibly hard to dig deep and find the "thing" I could dedicate my time to. I never ever thought of myself as a procrastinator and yet here I was staring at it on a daily basis, writing the same plans over and over again in the hope that one day, a spark of inspiration will motivate me to just move!

I hid behind other people and built their businesses and their business plans, helping them to secure millions of pounds of funding. I even taught people how to build their own communities and gave away so many ideas, I have lost count. I was giving everything I had to help other people and watch them embark on their successes, whilst I still sat in the shadow of mine.

It became evident as I threw myself into work, the feeling of pride was short lived. I would receive a nagging feeling inside of me which reminded me that all of this work enabled me to hide behind somebody else. I have always gained so much from any work I undertake, no matter if I am managing a team, training or writing an investment plan. I learn so much and I always like to think that I can take those learnings and use them over and over again. The difference however is to recognise when you are falling into a pattern which doesn't serve you or your highest good.

Last year, during the course of a 3 week period, our 3rd attempt at selling our house, fell through, 2 days before exchange. One week later I discovered that I was no longer needed at my job. The following week the business relationship I had been working on dissolved so quickly, I couldn't catch my breathe. Every single ending created another scar, another moment where I needed to dig a little deeper to find the good in everything I understood and believed to be true.

Yet something felt so different with these changes. When JFTP closed, my whole world closed in on me and for almost two years I hid, embarrassed, ashamed, not quite sure how to show up in the world. JFTP defined who I was and without it, I didn't recognise the person looking back at me. Yet this time, the courage and strength I found during my darkest days, surfaced so quickly and without further thought I started to gain momentum. I started to reach out to ask for recommendations, I started to actively look for a new role and more importantly I started to recognised that my love for business burned straight through me. I wanted to build again. Above all else, when I stared into the mirror, I knew exactly who stared back at me, I valued the person I had become, I knew the values I stood for and with grace I accepted I still had much to learn.

When life throws a few lemons, I always look to the stars. I am mindful of the signs around me, I often notice angel numbers, 1111, 1818, 1919, all of which always suggest change, the right path and gentle encouragement to keep moving forward, even if the days feel as still as a millpond. My intuition is heightened during these times as I actively seek assurance from the universe that somehow despite the turmoil, I will find my way through.

If I scroll through Facebook or Instagram, all of a sudden there are posts full of quotes, which I feel are talking directly to me, constantly reassuring and guiding. I know quotes are often overused and everywhere you look there is another quote telling you to enjoy your life and waste not another minute in pursuing your dreams. I have always believed that quotes serve a purpose - to inspire, educate and reach people in the exact moment they may need a hug from the universe.

Given the state of the world around us and the constant flow of sad news, I think we are living through a perfect storm, where social good, our determination as humans to stand up for what we believe and our desire to connect globally, alongside a really good quote or two might just be the tonic to remind us to look for joy in every moment. Words and stories will always find a way to our hearts, our everyday moments are founded on the stories we create for ourselves. Quotes are a gentle reminder to show up as our authentic selves and to know that we are surrounded by an enormous amount of love and support, should we ever need to call upon it.

My instincts tend to scream the loudest at me, when I am doing something that is so far off balance to what I want to do. Losing my job, the house sale and the business proposition, should have knocked me off my feet, instead I took it as a sign from the Universe to step up and do what I was meant to do. I should also mention that we didn't have any available money to start anything new, we were selling things on ebay and local selling sites just to make sure we could meet the current months financial commitments. I was producing 100's of online business evaluations to generate additional income. Yet amongst it all I knew what I needed to do, I needed to "find a product I loved and sell it"

Finding the product wasn't the tricky part. I had procrastinated over several during the past 2 years. I also knew the market, it was the very market I had learnt over and over during the 6 years I had grown JFTP. Selling the product would however mean marketing and marketing would require a budget. I was under no illusion, I knew to launch anything successfully online, you need a great product or service and traffic. The days of explosive organic growth were in the past, online businesses need a clear marketing strategy, which places community at the heart, linking all assets, from Facebook to Instagram to Email Lists and Podcasts and Websites and Funnels. Customers need to identify with you, in exchange for their precious time. The only asset I had, which I had protected fiercely during the past few years, was the community I had built.

I had played with my Facebook page on and off for the 6 months prior, deleting and tidying content. The page was unpublished and I knew nobody could see what I was doing. I was hiding and I recognised that. I hadn't imagined ever re-opening my platform, in all honesty it frightened me, I didn't know what was waiting for me and I had worked so hard to heal and protect the new life I had built.

Yet I also knew who I was and the values I held. I had the courage and strength inside of me to deal with anything that crossed my path.

I have come to trust that I have everything I need inside of me to overcome any obstacle in front of me. During the past 42 years, my inner strength has shown itself over and over and in perfect timing, things have always shown up as they should.

I am a passionate believer that our greatest gifts lie inside of us, we just need to create the space to allow ourselves to trust life's flow, which can often be challenging when you have a mortgage to pay and food to buy for your babies. I have found that the harder I worry and push on things to happen, the bigger the wall I seem to need to climb. If I can find a way to relax into the situation and release the resistance, a new job advert will suddenly appear in my inbox or somebody might suddenly need the services of my agency. Everything suddenly seems to find a way to flow. I may not always understand the reasons why sudden, unexpected diversions appear, I can however choose the way I respond to the situation and if need be, to recover as quickly as possible.

Re-opening my page was an extremely calm experience, I didn't give it too much thought, I just clicked unpublished on my phone and launched the Kindness Company as I picked up a pair of Alice's shoes off the floor and turned off my phone. It always makes me smile when I reflect back and realise that the most significant moments in my life happen at the point where there is no resistance. The universe can be pretty magical like that.

The months that have followed have surpassed my expectations. Community engagement has reached the 5 million mark, our new handmade dolls are creating smiles around the world, It is so amazing to see the platforms filled with kindness and love towards to each other, a stark contrast to what filled the posts from a few years ago. It seems everything can heal with time, the key is showing up as your authentic self and running your business from your heart.

We live in a time where we have the world at our fingertips. It has never been so easy to start a business. When I started JFTP, I used a photo of a teepee I had made Alice to kick start the platform. I didn't invest in stock or have things fully worked out. With the Kindness Company, I started the business using photos of the dolls we had made. I didn't have stock or a big production line mapped out in front of me.

However this time, I had experience. I knew the exact path I had to walk. The Kindness Company website was built over the course of a Saturday afternoon, 3 weeks after opening the platform, using free online software. A stark contrast to the £100k website built and designed for JFTP. As our beautiful dolls started to find new homes around the world I re-invested the money to upgrade the website and buy new supplies to reduce our costs, which I then handed back to our customers by reducing the price of the dolls. I still continue to build the business one brick at a time.

I also made sure that I had a steady income, very similar to the full time job I held down during the first 18 months as I built JFTP. I wanted to ensure that there weren't any pressures on the business. It was too new to carry the weight of needing to fund our financial commitments, no matter how big or small they were.

More importantly, I feel so incredibly happy. Nothing has ever felt more right than this. Business is a part of who I am. I missed the community and the business I had built and invested 6 years of my life into. It is so freeing to be back and posting and connecting with people around the world again.

I also lead with my intuition. I take the time to think things through rather than act on impulse. If I sense that something doesn't feel right, I will walk away, confident that what is meant to exist in my world will show up as it is meant to. I am really proud to have a resistance free rule.

I chose the name, The Kindness Company, as I wanted to bring into the world a value I believe with my whole being. To be kind. It is a 4 letter word which means so much and can create such a significant impact. I will never ever forget the kindness shown to me when I needed it the most, I will never forget Gill or Denise or my mum, who showed up for me in their own unique ways, helping me to find my way through. I won't forget the random phone calls to check that I was ok, even when I tried to push them away, or the wonderful tarot readings, when Denise wasn't quite sure how to tell me what was unfolding.

That said I take nothing for granted. The Kindness Company is very new, despite the size of the platform that she sits on and as with all small businesses she needs to be looked after and nurtured.

It's fun knowing the days are filled with working on my businesses full time again. It's even more exciting knowing that the future is my hands, shaped by the goals I want to achieve and the mark I want to leave on this world.

Chapter 7: Finding my way back

"We must be willing to let go of the life we planned, so as to have the life that is waiting for us"

Everyday for almost 12 months I would catch the ferry and cross the beautiful solent to travel to work. Water is always so calming and despite the occasional bobbing on the waters, I always feel completely relaxed. It was amazing to appreciate the joy I felt, It was such a lovely way to start my day.

One day I was walking past a giant building on the way to catch a taxi and I caught a glimpse of myself in the reflection of the glass, it brought such a huge smile to my face. The moment was completely perfect in the strangest of ways. I always imagined perfect moments to be surrounded by the most amazing, tranquil setting, cloudless skies reflected in the gorgeous water below. The intensity of the moment creating this perfect moment in time where you feel truly you. In reality those perfect moments can happen at any time, anywhere and sometimes with somebody you could never imagine.

At that moment I caught a glimpse of my 41 year old self, the smile on my face, the gentle beating of my heart, the serenity I felt, creating a "moment" where I could acknowledge that the person looking back at me in this oversized mirror, I liked, with all of my curves and bumps, I admired for the storm I had weathered and I loved deeply. This moment had crept up on me, it. was such a surprise. Every day for the past 2 years I have worked hard to understand my values, my passion and worked even harder to ensure that the person looking back at me in the mirror is somebody I could happily show up in the world as. That person not only needed to be a role model to my Alice but also somebody I could trust and depend on as I embarked on the next phase of my life.

I love holding a conversation with anybody who is willing to engage. I always find great healthy discussions fill me up. I love listening to people share stories and explain their childhood, present hood, what they hope for the future and anything and everything in between. The best conversations I always find seem to be about life experiences, the stories we tell each other. How amazing is that? to have the opportunity to be invited into somebody else's view of the world?

When I travelled away from home during my months of reset, I was so incredibly blessed to be surrounded by a group of kind, generous and brilliant people. During the day we were all onsite as consultants, in the evening our time was our own. The best conversations would last until 1am, often over a pink gin or two, it softened the ache I felt from being away from home.

One of the loveliest people I met was Jiri, a very kind, well travelled and incredibly smart human. Jiri would share his view of the world when we all hung out for dinner, he would tell tales of his travels around the world, which would occasionally involve a Honda and a hitch hiking story or two. His stories always made me laugh so much, the memory of them still make me smile to this day. We shared a love for food and he encouraged me to try new things. I fell in love with oysters, tapas, Indian food and soft shell crab, I came out in meat sweats when we all tried a 36oz steak.

Through it all I fell back in love with being in the company of others. I no longer had any reason to hide and slowly over the 6 months we all hung out, my confidence crept back. I would happily show up anywhere I was invited. There were perfect moments everywhere I looked, I just had to keep my eyes open and my heart full.

Jiri and I would chat about the lovely country of Czech and the effects the end of communism had on him growing up. It fascinated me. Jiri's zest for life, his fascination with adventure and his excitement to try new things, was such a blessing to me. His patience and time, helped to re-open my eyes and in doing so I started to realise that I had so much more adventure left inside of me. I could step back out into the world and build another business, I could travel more, I could try new food and allow myself to experience every day perfect moments. I recognised that I was starting to bounce back and somehow I had moved forward. The Universe had gifted me so much.

During my time of reset the universe had perfectly lined up a brilliant company to work for with a group of people who were loyal and so kind. Their generosity and their ability to accept me for who I am, without judgement helped me to regain both my strength and confidence. My heart is so full with the memories of these days away from home. I don't think Jiri ever realised the impact he had on me and how his kindness inspired me by simply being himself. I hope he will always travel through life telling stories and showing up as himself.

I find it amazing how we can heal our hearts and nurture our soul. How every cloud has a rainbow. Every tear we shed becomes the very water we splash around in when we sing, dance and laugh as we exist within this world.

Perfect moments aren't created by an expectation that something has to happen, they aren't created by other people, or by your surrounding. They are created the very moment you can exist at peace with everything that has been, an acceptance of where you are now and an excitement for the road ahead. Perfect moments exist within you. They are your gift for weathering a storm and having had the courage to face yourself and deepen your incredible strength.

Have you heard of the expression "You are a people person" I always smile when I hear it used to describe somebody, it is an expression I have heard many people use to describe me. In broad terms it means that you have the ability to engage others. I also think it means that you have the ability to be empathetic and can understand the language of body and expression.

Do you often find yourself in situations where people you may never have met before suddenly start sharing secrets or intimate details about themselves? My husband always laughs at me, when I explain how I met a person on a train or a ferry or even standing in the que and within 10 minutes I know how many children they have or that a spouse has passed away recently, I normally see a picture or two as well. He finds it very strange that somebody can be so open with a stranger.

The other day I was sitting happily in the back of an Uber chatting away and somehow the conversation drifted to the bumps in the road. The lovely driver taught me why the roads were bumpy and explained how they need to be resurfaced to reinforce their strength to cope with the increased loads the trucks and cars bring with them. I have no idea how I found all of this out, he wanted to share and I was more than happy to listen.

Funnily enough these conversations have led to so many unexpected perfect moments.

Chapter 8: God.. The Universe .. Is anybody up there?

"Follow your bliss and the Universe will open doors where there were only walls"

Joseph Campbell

Ever since I was a little girl I had this notion that something beyond us, lived within the clouds. Maybe it was my greek grandmother, who, without fail attended church every Sunday. Her faith held her together like glue. Maybe it was the secret prayers I used to make when I was a small little girl and I wanted the hurt in our home to stop.

If I am honest, I am not too sure where the notion of God within my life came from. The school I attended was predominantly white, other than R.E lessons, I generally wasn't exposed to different cultures or religions. That would come later when I entered Uni and I found myself as one of 3 white girls in a business technology degree at Kingston, full of boys from varying cultures. I once remember being told that "I was ok, as I wasn't really white" to say I was confused is an understatement. I had no idea who I was or what I wanted to be when I "grew up" I just followed the path that was laid in front of me.

I often try to explain to Alice, that education is a gift. I explain that around the world there are millions of girls who haven't the opportunity to go to school, or know how to read or write. We have been given a gift to use our voice, to be able to write and share stories, to read to expand our knowledge. I wanted Alice to know that she has an opportunity every day to choose how she responds to the opportunities in front of her. She may feel afraid at times, but stepping forward will not only honour her, but the millions of children around the world who dream of a better life.

As I grew older and I met Clive, I discovered that not everybody had a belief. My husband is a self-proclaimed atheist. I tend to default to giving people space when I am not sure what to think of something. We have been together for over 20 years and I can honestly say that we haven't ever argued about religion or beliefs. Clive allows me the space to figure things out, even if that means my head is often buried in books or reading articles. He provides me with the space to throw my arms up in frustration when I just cant seem to put the pieces together. The only time the topic of religion has cropped up, was a short while after Alice was born and we had a discussion around a christening. It seemed the done thing to do. Everybody we knew, was christening their babies, choosing godparents and holding celebrations.

However, it didn't ever sit right with us, to choose a path for Alice, when she was too small to decide for herself and whilst I believe that we all have a level of protection, I do not believe that christening my child would have been the deal breaker between deciding if she was protected or not. And so we approached it as we did with everything else, we chose to do things our way and enable Alice to choose for herself as she gets older.

As the years have passed I have to admit if I read anything which referenced God, I would squirm. It made me feel so uncomfortable. I genuinely didn't know what I thought, what I believed. It was such a huge source of discomfort I turned a blind eye, I decided bumbling along was probably the best course of action.

When my world fell away from under my feet there was a moment when I stood still and secretly prayed that somebody was out there. I realised that I wanted to hold onto a faith which was bigger than myself.

Why else would there be pain?

Why else would all of these things happen? there had to be a reason and there it was again, the need to delve a little deeper into my soul and find what connects us.

I can honestly say that spending the time to explore different religions and ask myself what I really thought about God was one of the most satisfying experiences. It's truly fascinating. I was captivated at the idea that every religion is founded on the same belief, it has just evolved into a different form or a different name over time. I knew I believed something, I just didn't know what it was.

My beliefs have formed over time, they have been created through some extremely tough moments, moments when I questioned the precious life I have been given. I believe what I believe because every belief makes sense to me. It doesn't matter if the only person they ever make sense to, is me. I am ok with that. I have arrived at the conclusion that there is much that lives beyond the clouds, rainbows always make me smile, I listen for the sound of the birds as its natures way of saying hi. I look out for pretty flowers as its the universes way of showing me there is more to the world than my eyes first see. What a gift, to be able to hear and see.

I am a huge believer that we are a result of our own actions. I believe that we have the power to change our future, I believe in the good in people and understand that circumstances can often dictate behaviour. I believe in the power of the mind and our ability to meet people exactly where they are at. I believe that we are responsible for the way that we feel, I believe that we have an ego which often tells us we can't do something. I believe more than anything in trusting and following my intuition. I believe in love and friendship and surrounding yourself with people who fill you up with joy. I believe you can turn a frown upside down and a laugh a day will always keep the doctor away. I believe in the human spirit and our souls needs to grow to enable us to reach our next level of human. I believe in choice and freedom and speaking up for those who cant. I believe in Kindness and that It should always be the foundation from which we build friendships, love and even business from. I believe in the power of experience and the lessons that fall from those experiences. I believe that the path in front of us, is ours and ours alone. I believe in the vulnerability of the human spirit, I believe in the stars and angels and the universe.

And so what do I think of God? I think that something exists which is intangible to us. Call it God, Buddha or Allah or even the Universal Laws. I genuinely do believe that we can all identify with God in the best way that suits who we are.

My hubby doesn't believe in the Universal laws, he doesn't understand why at some of my darkest and lightest moments I reach for tarot cards. He doesn't understand why I am constantly asking him to reframe something negative into a positive, or why I have an obsession to see the good in all that is in front of me.

But he does respect who I am and he gives me the space to figure things out in my own way. He stands by when I chat to Alice about the universe and I support her with her journal writing. I will never preach, but if I am asked a question I will answer it as truthfully as I can.

I love my values and I love the fact that I am passionate about so many things. I love the fact that for the first time in my life I have a foundation to build the rest of my life upon, I can navigate my feelings and reach for better thoughts if the day feels a little grey, I have the confidence to know that I have everything I ever need inside of me.

Chapter 9: Saying Goodbye

"The only question in life is whether or not you are going to answer a hearty 'YES!' to your adventure"

Joseph Campbell

Selling our beautiful home was a decision Clive and I had to make at the exact time we decided to place JFTP Into Voluntary Liquidation. As a director I had taken out several personal guarantees which were secured against our home, without a business, a salary or anyway of knowing what the future held, we had to offer up our home to the loan companies in order to settle what was owed. I believed at the time that the liquidation would offer a path for reimbursement for our customers, selling our home would resolve the monies owed to the various loan companies.

It is perfectly normal for a director of a business to be asked to use their home as security. Every director I know, has had to do the same and whilst it is a source of worry, you never really think you will be placed in a position where you will have to sell your home to recoup losses. Over the years of trading I had taken out several loans to support the business, in the absence of investor support, every loan had been paid back. I didn't think for a moment that this situation would be any different.

Due to the size of JFTP and the strength of my credit rating, we secured over £250k of loans against our home. An amount which now makes my eyes water. At the time, I just remember feeling strangled by everything that the business was going through aswell as a huge feeling of responsibility to do the right thing, I felt I had no choice.

The decision to place JFTP into voluntary liquidation was by no means easy. We had to consider our customers and the payment plans they were playing into, we had to consider our team and the fact that they would also lose their jobs and we had to consider that we would need to sell our home in order to settle the monies due.

Often when a company liquidates, the lender will ask you to continue to re-pay the monies owed. Unfortunately the damage online against my personal reputation left many scars and nobody would offer me any type of employment. In truth I also wasn't sure what I wanted to do. I was deeply unhappy, I had no idea how to navigate the future.

Our house went on the market immediately, we offered it as a token to the loan companies and asked them to be patient and allow us to sell the house and repay the amounts due. For two years, I would find weekly emails in my inbox from the loan companies, threatening me with bankruptcy, demanding payment. It was an ongoing battle. I would find myself in court several times, faced with a judge who didn't believe that we were willing to sell. We had reduced the price of the house by almost £200k. Brexit hadn't helped as it was becoming increasingly difficult to sell. Over the course of 2 years we faced 3 failed sales, just days before exchange. Each failed exchange accrued solicitor costs and interest from each of the lenders.

During this time I had no choice but to step up and face the situation head on. I was very used to burying my head in the sand, isolating myself and during the earlier months, this was exactly how I behaved. However as time passed I found a way to reclaim my power and own the conversation. There were times where I was accused of being dishonest or attempts were made to make me feel as if I were worth nothing, it was incredibly humiliating.

To hold a job where you fight with people every single day, as these lawyers did, requires a certain degree of cynicism. One of the lenders once explained to me that assuming the worst in a person was the only way they could all sleep at night. To say that it bothered me, was an understatement. When the threats started to become more venomous something very strange happened. It literally stopped bothering me, I had found myself disconnecting from the emotion around the situation.

As each sale failed, I prepared to hand back the keys to the mortgage company. I had made peace that if we reached that point, I would be comfortable to hand back the keys to the bank. It was our worst possible situation and I faced it head on. We were also very clear with everybody, I didn't want to play games, I didn't want to fight. I just wanted to settle what was owed in order to allow us to move on with our lives.

When news came through that there was a 4th sale, we were also facing a repossession order from two companies at the time. The loan companies had lost their patience and were now arguing amongst each other. The judge had granted a date - September 24th. In order for the sale to be allowed to continue, we would have to exchange prior to this date. It was an impossible ask, to race ahead with yet another sale in 6 weeks.

As I sit here and type and this, I am not sure how we managed it. The pressure was immense, the fighting between the loan companies heightened, solicitors began making up numbers and tried to go back on agreements we had made regarding the amounts they would be paid. At every step I tried my best to remain calm, however it did take its toll. The idea that we would lose our home to repossession and at worst bankruptcy didn't sit well with me. I just didn't believe that throughout the journey we had travelled, throughout everything we had learnt, we would fall at the last hurdle.

I sought help from the tarot cards, I reached out to the universe and I tried with every fibre in my body to push forward. I set aside the temptation to argue back, to try and defend myself. I had come too far to let myself down at the last hurdle. Everything I had learnt during these past 2 years prepared me for one of our biggest battles against some of the toughest people I have ever met. They tested every skill I had.

The final lender argued with us about the final amounts due to them until 5pm the night before completion. My solicitor was asking me to make a decision, the chain would have to be informed if the sale was to fail, the impact would be further significant financial losses. I just wouldn't let it fail, the fire in my belly told me to keep going, to maintain communication and deal only with the facts, ensuring to remove all emotion. In the end, after a flurry of emails, a concession was reached and we ended the day at 5pm confirming that the sale would progress the following day.

On October 19th at 11am, I received a phone call, I can honestly say I never ever thought I would receive. Completion had taken place and our beautiful home had been sold to a lovely family, who I knew would love it as much as we did. As soon as the phone call had ended, emails started to flood my inbox, payments were leaving our solicitors and confirmations were being sent to each of the lenders. I sat staring at my screen, watching in disbelief as £250,000 was sent out to clear our final financial commitments.

The enormity of what had happened hit me an hour later when I spontaneously burst into tears. I felt such huge relief within my body. I had done it! I had seen everything through to the very last moment and everybody had been paid. My solicitor told me that she hadn't seen anybody hang on and fight the way I had, our wonderful estate agent told me that it was a testament to my personality.

In reality it was a testament to the person I had grown into. I had chosen to fight, I had chosen to stand up and fight for what I knew to be right and I very much wanted to honour the commitments I had made. It was so incredibly important to me that I kept my word to the lenders, to our solicitors and to everybody involved. I had removed all fear from the situation by facing up to the very thing that had frightened me - repossession. I looked at it straight in the eye and gave it a very respectful wink, "I see you" and in doing so, I knew I had everything I needed inside of me to see this through to the very end. The aggression from the lenders, whilst upsetting didn't impact me the way it once did.

26 months after the journey had started, we were finally able to close our chapter. What started as a path through darkness, countless twist and turns and stunning highs and lows, we had survived. We are finally free and happy. There is a peace in my heart I haven't ever known before. As a little girl I fought every single day for a life different to the one I was born into, I fought to change the generational cycle for my little girl, I fought for Alice during 2 cycles of IVF, I fought for my business for 6 years. The biggest fight I eventually fought was for myself.

In the end the journey had broken my heart in order to heal my soul. The Universe had a plan all along and whilst I fought and resisted at times, I now understand that it had always supported me. I have met the most amazing people on the way. For the first time in my adult life, I have friends who I love dearly. I give without ever wanting anything in return, I lead with the same passion that fills me up. And I can love with my whole heart, the heartache I used to feel has disappeared, the cracks have healed and whilst the scars are still there, I have much respect for the journey that helped them to mend.

Chapter 10: The Long Journey Home

"The privilege of a lifetime is being who you are"
Joseph Campbell

For the first time in our lives, we are debt free and even though we didn't walk away with anything from the sale, I can fall asleep at night incredibly happy and content. Most importantly, through it all we have remained as a family. The love I feel for both Clive and Alice is indescribable. They have been my strength and whilst the image of my 6 year old girl patting me on the back telling me "shushh, don't cry mummy" is incredibly real in my mind, I know that showing her that I can bounce back is the biggest lesson I could ever share with her. We all want our children to be proud of us, in some ways we want them to know everything we have been through in order to protect them and prevent them from ever having to go through something similar.

However I have come to learn, If I am proud of myself, everything that comes from that, will show Alice how to show up in the world as her best self. As a little girl, she doesn't fully understand the journey of the past 2 years, however she has taken everything in her stride. When her teachers tell Clive and I that she is a credit to us, they have no idea what that actually means. They have no idea how hard we fought to keep her world as stable as possible, even if that meant we went without. They have no idea of the things we sold to keep her at her school to ensure her education remained steady or even why we moved shortly after putting our home on the market.

Protecting Alice was at the heart of every decision we made. I couldn't be prouder of the young lady she has grown into and whilst finding her voice has been confusing at times, I know that by simply using it in the right way, she will turn up in this world as her incredible self.

Clive throughout everything has remained my rock. We have argued and thrown words around, but we are bound together so tightly. I always wondered how somebody so quiet with such different interests could love somebody like me. I am everything he isn't.

We have survived because Clive is my biggest cheerleader. During the nights when I would cry he would let me, he didn't molly coddle me and pretend things would be ok. His strength is in the fact that he sees the reality in situations and for that I am incredibly grateful. He has never ever blamed me. He has never accused me of letting my family down, even if at times it felt that I had. He has enabled me and given me the space to figure things out. I am not even sure how he sat by for months and months, when our finances had dried up and gave me the space to curl up and cry. Though I do remember the very poignant statement "no more self help shit Ef" and that was the sign, the sign to move on and stop procrastinating and take a leap of faith.

Our marriage isn't perfect, but it's perfect for us. When you have seen each other at your absolute worst, where else can you possibly go, but forward. It would have been so easy to walk away, the key was not to give up on each other. My husband will have my heart forever, we have grown into each other. As we celebrate our 20th anniversary, I am so excited to grow old together, simply because I know we can.

As I look ahead I am not sure what the future will hold. The Kindness Company is growing every day and impacting millions of people around the world. My agency is growing from strength to strength and I have finally sat down and written a book I have been trying to write in my head since I was a little girl. The cycle is complete and the next one is now beginning. I am so excited for the path ahead, for everything it will teach me and for the new life we are creating. I am excited to watch Alice grow up, I have much admiration for the young women she is developing into. Her strength and her resolve to do the right thing, warms my heart. Watching her step out into the world and use her voice fills me with such pride. We are raising a bright, strong spirited little girl who is just starting to understand the power of her mind. I think I was always meant to fight for her and become her mummy and she was always meant to be my little girl.

When I started out on this journey to write this book, I genuinely thought it would sit in a drawer and gather dust. I am 42 years old and whilst I hope that there is plenty of time in front of me, I am not prepared to throw away precious time hoping I will find the courage to try something new. Every day is a gift and I want to show up and create the life that I want to live, on my terms. Business will always be a huge passion of mine. I fundamentally believe that business has the ability to change the world and if not the whole world, certainly a piece of it. Entrepreneurs are some of the most amazing people on the planet, they will go on to create impact, simply because they are bold enough to believe they can.

Do what you love, because of the impact it can create, the example it will set and the amazing lessons it will teach you.

Self Care is hugely important too. Especially as the evenings can remind me that I no longer have the stamina I used to have. But with all of that, I open my eyes each day happy and excited for the day ahead, often with a renewed energy which can only come from showing up and doing what I love everyday.

Choose your adventure, trust your path and follow your heart. There is a reason we have been given a mind to think for ourselves, instincts to guide us and a heart to love with. Fill your world with every piece of goodness that you can. If the challenges ahead feel bleak, I promise you with every part of my being, the reward for seeing it through will surpass anything you have ever experienced before. If I had given up, I wouldn't be sitting here typing this, I wouldn't be getting ready to take Alice to her first sleepover or thinking about date night with my hubby. Defining yourself in your current moment will impact the path ahead, take a deep breath and stand back and know that everything you feel now, is temporary. Don't waste your lessons, use them! empower people with them, show the world who you are. But most of all, be kind. Kindness is the one gift we all have to give, no matter our age or our beliefs. It is a basic, but very special value and if you use it the joy that will emulate from it will create a ripple effect for years to come.

Choose Kindness above everything else. Choose to help and support another person, to spring a surprise on them, to stand up for somebody when they are unable to stand up for themselves. Kindness is magical, it wraps us up in a cloak of invisibility and makes us feel good inside. It softens the hardest of blows and attracts the most amazing people into our lives.

Be Kind, is a phrase I use often, it was coined during a period in my life when I was in desperate need of it. A random phone call or text, an email, they all meant so much.

Kindness reminds you that you are remembered, that you are loved. We are all here on this earth to experience our own journey, you will never truly understand what goes on inside a person or behind a smile. Kindness is our human way to extend a piece of ourselves, to create a ripple effect far beyond what our eyes can see.

In a world where we can type faster than the thoughts flowing in our mind, hate has never been so prevalent. That said nor has Kindness or love. When there is a battle or an impact to the way we want to live our lives, we stand together, we choose love, we form an invisible bond and as Iron Man said "form a suit of armour around the world"

The squares we see on Instagram, the feeds we see online, have started to form our life story. Every picture we post, every word we write, forms part of the legacy we want to leave behind. We are sharing a part of who we are, in the hope that somewhere out there, somebody will read what we have written, look to the picture we have posted and feel inspired to reach for more. I am a massive believer that the rate of technological change we have experienced over the years, was designed to come together at this exact moment in time. Our generation was chosen to grow these incredible platforms, to evolve humanity to it's next level for the next generation ahead.

Kindness permeates and breaks down the barriers we have built. Isn't it strange that we are using kindness to break down the very things we have built out of fear. Kindness is fear's nemesis. It always has been.

Be kind, not for kindness sake, but for the sake of another human being. Give somebody you know a virtual cuddle, send flowers, pick up the phone, send that funny emoji. Remind somebody that they matter, that the friendship or relationship you have means something. Pick up the phone when it rings, even when you feel most tiered. Your words, your voice, matter and somebody out there needs to hear them from you.

One of things I promised myself when I hit the big reject button on my life, was to choose values which I could embody. Values which would matter to me and I hoped would help me to show up in this world as my true self. Be Kind has become my motto. My company is called The Kindness Company for a reason. The dolls we have created have shown up in the feeds of 5 million people and I truly hope that when you see them, you smile. When you smile, everybody else smiles with you and sometimes that smile can start from a pretty doll stuffed with organic stuffing, created from a place of joy and inspired by imagination.

As Alice has started to get older, I have been reminded of the young girls bickering that often filled my school years. Part of growing up is understanding how to resolve conflict, how to see another's point of view. Childhood is one of our hardest adventures, thoughts are running wild as you learn a hundred things and without the emotional maturity to understand them - yet! You can't quite place how you feel or often understand the difference between yourself and somebody else. The piece of advice I can offer my little girl is this..

"Before you say anything in anger, ask yourself "Am I being Kind?"

Even at such a young age, a little girl or a little boy can cause hurt. They emulate the adults and the world around them. They carry the hurt and trauma we have experienced in our lives, they hear our words, they feel what we feel, they use their eyes to see. We need to remind ourselves that taking care of ourselves will help not only us, but the generation in front of us.

Be Kind wasn't something I grew up with. It wasn't the world that surrounded me. I was born into a lot of hate and anger. I witnessed pain at a level that no 5 year old little girl should ever have to see. I spent Christmas days in hospital, holding my mum, simply because I had no choice. But now, I recognise that Kindness can manifest in many ways. I choose Kindness above everything else.

Kindness saved my life and that isn't something I mean metaphorically. It literally saved my life. It was a hug from my then 6 year old who reminded me that the life I have been given is precious. The people who I had allowed to place me into the corner, the loss of everything I knew, facing the person I absolutely hated in the mirror, it had taken its toll. And whilst the thought of Alice cuddling me and telling me that she loves me, should never have been placed on my little girl, she saved my life. Nowadays I spring out of bed and chase her around the house trying to squeeze her and kiss her, amongst the teenage grunts of "get off me" I laugh from the depths of my soul, she is an absolutely amazing human and I have the privilege of being her mummy, with front row seats as to how she will lead the life she has been given.

Kindness is simple, it is part of who we are. It is one of our fundamental qualities. How lucky are we that we can give it so freely. How lucky are we that we can show up at any moment we choose and be present for somebody. Use the arms you have been given, extend a hug, use your voice and support another, use the skills you have been given and create an impact on a world that is craving for a touch of kindness.

I wish you much love, health and happiness for the incredible life that is yours to lead. I wish you much success, but most of all I wish you a journey which will inspire you and help you to find so much joy.
Be you!
Thats the only person you can be.
There just isn't time to be anybody else.

The future is exactly where it should be. Ahead. Its time for the next adventure …

"If you speak to somebody at the level of the mind, then you speak to the mind.

If you speak from your heart, you will speak to their heart.

But if you speak from experience and life is your story, you will change lives"

Deepak Chopra

Want to hear more from Effie?

Keep up to date with all of the latest news at:

 @joineffiemoss

 @effiemoss

 @effiemoss

www.effiemoss.com

Explore The Kindness Company

Keep up to date with all of the latest news at:

 @sprinklealittlekindness

 @sprinklealittlekindness

www.thekindnesscompany.co.uk